BRIDGEWAYS

Group Style 2

English Conversation

-Learning English Has Never Been So Easy-

HAKMUNSA.com

머리말

학생들이 영어회화 시간에 대화 학습 활동을 할 때에는 4~5명 단위의 소그룹으로 편성하는 것이 효과적입니다. 영어회화를 가르치는 교사는 학생들이 교실에서의 대화 진행 활동에 적극적으로 참여하지 않는다고 신경을 쓰며 걱정 할 것은 못됩니다.
학생들이 골고루 돌아가며 대화에 참여할 수 있는 균등한 기회가 주어 질수 있도록 대화 진행 분위기를 조성해 주는 것이 무엇보다 중요합니다.
소그룹 편성시 유의할 점은 우선 학생들이 서로 편안하게 느끼는 대화상대 3~4명씩 서로 선택할 수 있도록 하여 학생들의 대화 참여 기회를 증가시켜 주게 해야 합니다.
또 그룹 중의 한명은 보다 능력 있는 학생 1명씩 반드시 배정하여 주는 것도 중요한 진행 방침입니다.
왜냐하면 그렇게 함으로써 다른 학생들은 좀더 능력 있는 자로부터 배울 수 있으며 보다 진전된 회화를 할 수 있어 학생들이 실제로 대화 기회를 적극적으로 증가 시켜 줍니다.
이렇게 해서 더 미숙한 학생들이 좀 더 능력 있는 이들로부터 배울 수 있는 가능성을 높이고 그룹원들이 좀 더 조화롭게 어울릴 수 있는 분위기를 조성할 수 있게 됩니다.

게다가 이책은 원어민의 "일상언어" 습득에도 참여할 수 있는 기회를 배려하고 있습니다.
"일상생활언어"란 원어민들이 일상 생활에서 편안하게 사용하는 생활언어입니다. 우리 학생들은 영어 수업상의 교실영어 뿐만 아니라 실제 삶에서 사용되는 언어도 또한 배울수 있게 되어 해외여행에서 현지민의 일상생활을 더 잘 익힐 수 있도록 하게 될 것입니다.

First published 2008
HAKMUNSA.com
37-18 haengchon-dong Jongno-gu Seoul, korea
Tel 02-738-5118 Fax 02-725-8023
http://www.hakmun.co.kr

Price : ₩8,500

ISBN 978-89-5647-007-8
ISBN 978-89-5647-009-2(전3권)

BRIDGEWAYS

Group Style

2

Paul Z. Jambor

English Conversation

- Learning English Has Never Been So Easy -

HAKMUN PUBLISHING CO.

Author: **Paul Z. Jambor**

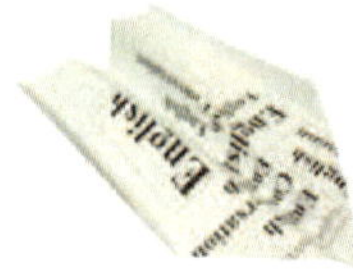

An EFL Book for Korean Learners of English

Bridgeways 2

Group Styled English Conversation

Learning English Has Never Been So Easy

Never has it been so easy to learn English conversation. It only takes a group of learners to utilize this book to get maximum results. That is to say, conversation can only be learned if the language is applied in real use, and what better way to do this than to take part in group conversation in contexts outlined by this book.

First published 2008

Seoul, Korea

http://www.hakmun.co.kr

Price: ₩13,000

ISBN: 978-89-467-8335-5

Foreword

It is important that students form small groups of 4-5 students as they facilitate conversation in the English Classroom. Teachers of English as a foreign language often complain that learners do not engage in oral conversational activities within their classrooms. What they may not realize is that it is often very challenging for learners to do so if the classroom is not set up so as to give the learners the opportunity to converse. It is best to place at least one 'more capable' learner within the group since it gives the other learners the opportunity to improve their conversational abilities. Also, it is a good idea to have learners choose their own groups in order to give them the chance to choose group members they feel most comfortable with. This dramatically increases the chances that learners will actually converse. Perhaps the best method is to pick the more capable learners ahead of time so they can pick 3-4 members they feel most at ease with. This increases the chances for group harmony and the likelihood that the weaker learners will learn from the more capable others.

What is more, this book exposes learners to some instances of 'casual language'. In essence, 'casual language' is language native speakers use in everyday situations. This allows learners to learn not only the English of the English class, but

Table of Contents

Unit	Topics	Pages
Unit 1 Getting to know you	• Introductions • Personal Interests • Asking for personal Information • Ways of saying hello and goodbye	p.8 - Getting to know one another p.9 - Introducing other people p.10 - Greetings and Leave-taking p.11 - Asking for Personal Information p.12 - Comprehension Activities p.13 - Writing Reinforcement p.14 - Puzzle
Unit 2 Day to Day	• Kinds of transportation for getting around • Asking others about the ways they commute • Asking others about their weekend plans • Asking people about their occupations	p.16 - Kinds of Transportation p.17 - Ways of getting around p.18 - Ways of Acknowledging p.19 - Occupations p.20 - Occupation Enquiries p.21 - Review Activities p.22 - Puzzle
Unit 3 On the Job	• Making general enquiries about work and school • How to express future aspirations • How to ask for reinforcement (Is that so?/ Are you sure?) • How to bring a conversation to an end	p.24 - Random Questions p.25 - I'd like to be a/an ... p.26 - Keeping a Conversation Going p.27 - Why do you like your job? p.28 - Active Listening p.29 - Review Activities p.30 - Puzzle
Unit 4 Eating Out	• Kinds of Restaurants • Types of foods • Ordering in restaurants • What's available on the menu	p.32 - Agreeing with Others p.33 - Making Food Choices p.34 - Agreement 'Expressions' p.35 - Expressing Regret p.36 - Listening Comprehension p.37 - Review Activities p.38 - Puzzle
Unit 5 Money	• Units of currency • Asking for change • Borrowing money • Asking others to make a purchase • Learning money related terms	p.40 - Asking for Change p.41 - Making Requests p.42 - Money Terms p.43 - Denominations of Money p.44 - Listening Comprehension p.45 - Review Activities p.46 - Puzzle

Unit	Topics	Pages
Unit 6 **Travelling and Getting Around**	• Transportation Terminology • Asking people about their travel plans • How to offer suggestions • Modes of transportation	p.48 - Taking the Ferry p.49 - Comprehension Activities p.50 - Travel Terminology p.51 - Travel Destinations p.52 - Comprehension Activities p.53 - Review Activities p.54 - Puzzle
Unit 7 **High-Tech Gadgets**	• High-Tech Terminology • Asking people whether they can use a certain High-Tech device • Asking for permission to use other people's High-Tech gadgets • High-Tech device usages and functions	p.56 - Entertainment Systems p.57 - Can you use a/an ..? p.58 - High-Tech Terminology p.59 - Could I use your ..? p.60 - Comprehension Activities p.61 - Review Activities p.62 - Puzzle
Unit 8 **Entertainment**	• Entertainment Terminology • The kinds of games and consoles • Movie Genres • Selecting the right movies	p.64 - Movie Titles and Genres p.65 - Video Games and Consoles p.66 - Entertainment Terminology p.67 - Entertainment Choices p.68 - Comprehension Activities p.69 - Review Activities p.70 - Puzzle
Unit 9 **Daily Exercise**	• Exercise related terminology • How to express the preference of one thing over another • Inviting others to do exercise or to partake in sports • The various kinds of exercise	p.72 - Hard Work or Fun? p.73 - Tennis in the Park p.74 - Exercise Related Terms p.75 - Building Muscle p.76 - Comprehension Activities p.77 - Review Activities p.78 - Puzzle
Unit 10 **The Day After Tomorrow**	• The varieties of Future Tense • Future Tense Interrogatives • Talking about future events • Speaking in Future Tense	p.80 - Waiting for the bus p.81 - I'm going to go out p.82 - The Varieties of Tenses p.83 - I'm going to the market p.84 - Comprehension Activities p.85 - Review Activities p.86 - Puzzle

Unit 11 The Day Before Yesterday	• The Present Simple and The Present Progressive • How to talk about things that happened yesterday • Asking questions about past events • Things that happened some time ago	p.88 - Simple Past p.89 - Present Progressive p.90 - Past Tenses p.91 - Our holiday was nice p.92 - Comprehension Activities p.93 - Review Activities p.94 - Puzzle
Unit 12 Clothing and Accessories	• Fashion Accessories • The Conjunction 'But' • The Preposition 'With' • Giving and receiving assistance while shopping	p.96 - Fashion Accessories p.97 - Lending Money p.98 - Accessory Terms p.99 - Getting Some Assistance p.100 - Comprehension Activities p.101 - Review Activities p.102 - Puzzle
Hidden Tape Scripts	• Transcripts of conversations (Activity 11:b -T5) in each of the respective units	p.103
Puzzle Solutions	• Solutions to the puzzles at the end of each respective unit	p.110
Complementary Activity	• An additional activity that correlates to an activity within its respective unit	p.114
Supplementary Writing Activity	• An additional writing activity to gauge the learners' appreciation of the Bridgeways 2 course.	p.115
Irregular Verbs	• A list of irregular verbs and their past tenses	p.116
Guide to Using Bridgeways	**IMPORTANT!** • This section is required reading before learners start on Unit 1	p.118
Attention Teachers!	**IMPORTANT!** • All teachers should read this section before they start any lessons	p.121

BUSINESS NAME

Unit 1

Getting to Know You

In your free time.

Grammar

Content

- Simple Present
- Simple Present Interrogative

Unit breakdown:

Getting to Know Others	p. 8
Introducing Other People	p. 9
Greetings and Leave-taking	p.10
Asking for Personal Info.	p.11
Comprehension Activities	p.12
Writing Reinforcement	p.13
Puzzle	p.14

It's so nice to meet you.

This unit focuses on …

- Introductions
- Personal interests
- Asking for personal information
- Ways of saying hello and goodbye

I'm Yuki.
I'm Yoko.

1) Please allow me to introduce myself.

A) Hi, there.
B) Hello.

A) I am Yuki.
B) I'm Yoko.

A) Hi, Yoko. It's good to meet you.
B) It's good to meet you, too, Yuki.

Now practice the above conversation within your group. Use your own names while making up your own scenarios and say them out loud in English. Don't forget to involve all group members.

"It's a pleasure to meet you."

It's	good / nice / a pleasure / great	to	meet	you	.

It's	good / nice / a pleasure / great	to	meet	you	too	.

Now practice the above conversation within your group. Use your own names while making up your own scenarios and say them out loud in English. Don't forget to involve all group members.

3) Personal Interests T1 Listen to the Conversation

- **What do you like to do?**
- **I like to travel.**
- **What do you do?**
- **I am a teacher.**

4) Introducing other people.

A)

This	is	my	friend	John	.
She		our	sister	Wendy	
They	are	my	cousins	Paul and Steve	

B)

It's	great	to	meet	you	John	.
	nice				Wendy	
	wonderful				two	

C)

It's	good	to	meet	you	too	.
	nice					
	a pleasure					

Now practice the above conversation within your group. Use your own names while making up your own scenarios and say them out loud in English. Don't forget to involve all group members.

5) Listening Activity T2

A) Hi, Harry.

B) Hi, Brad.

A) Harry. This is my friend Thomas.

B) Hello Thomas. It's a pleasure to meet you.

C) It's a pleasure to meet you, too, Harry.

B) Do you live nearby?

C) No, I live in New York city. I'm here on a visit.

6) On the Weekends

Q What do you do on the weekends?

A I bike and hike with friends.

Q Where do you hike?

A On a mountain near my house. The mountain has a nice view.

Now practice the above conversation within your group. Use your own names while making up your own scenarios and say them out loud in English. Don't forget to involve all group members.

7) Greetings and Leave-taking

Now practice the above illustrated ways of greeting and leave-taking. It is important that you know how to use and understand all of them. Don't forget to involve all group members.

8: a) What do you do in your free time? T3

A) Hi, there.

B) Hello. How are you?

A) Good, thanks.
Janet. What do you do when you're not working?

B) I go to the beach. I like snorkeling in the coral reefs.

A) Really? That sounds great.

B) Yes, I think so, too. The fish there are really colorful.

Now practice the above conversation within your group. Use your own names and substitute the underlined information with your own words. Say your conversations out loud in English. Don't forget to involve all group members.

8: b) Personal Identity T4

A) Excuse me. What's your name?
B) My name is Diane Southerland.
A) Is Southerland your last name?
B) Yes, it is.
A) Can you spell that for me?
B) S-O-U-T-H-E-R-L-A-N-D
A) Thank you. Now can I have your phone number, please?
B) Yes, it's 0-1-2-4-5-6-7-8-9-0.
A) Thank you, Diane.
B) You are most welcome.

Bridgeways School of English
Diane Southerland
Teacher
Cell: 012-456-7890

9) How old are you?

In 2007

A) What's your name?
B) My name is Monica Black.
A) How old are you?
B) I'm 17 years old.
A) What is your student number?
B) It's B-9-8-7-4-5-6-3-2-1.
A) Thank you.
B) You're welcome.

Bridgeways School of English

Name: Monica Black
Birthday: July 3, 1990
Student Number: B– 987-456-321

"Can I have your student number?"

Now take the conversation and model your own conversations on it. Once again use your own information.

10) Fill in the missing information

Friend 1

Name: ____________________
Telephone: ____________________
Student number: ____________________
Age: __________ years old

Friend 2

Name: ____________________
Telephone: ____________________
Student number: ____________________
Age: __________ years old

Now take turns filling in the missing information on the student cards. Give your group members your personal data.

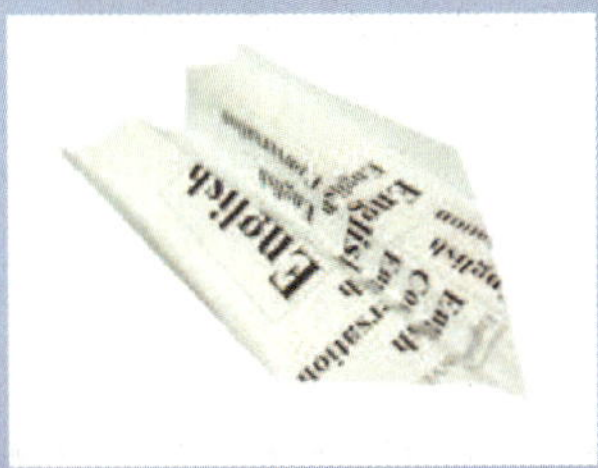

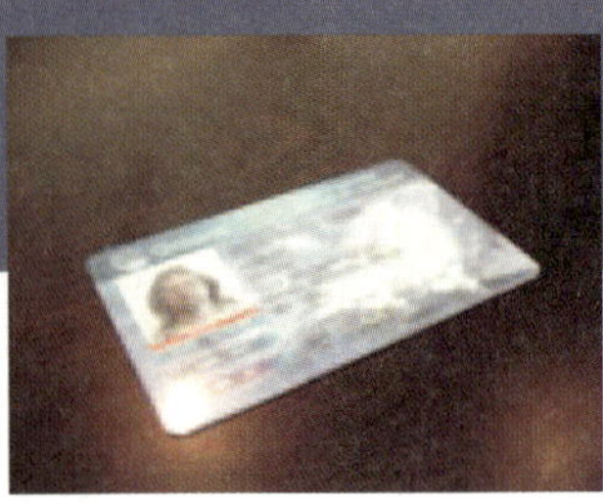

11: a) Fill in the missing information

Fill in the missing information by asking your group members for their personal data.

	Example	Friend 1	Friend 2	Friend 2
Name	Nari Choi			
First Name	Nari			
Last Name	Choi			
Student Number	123-987-456			
Age	12 years old			

A) What's your name?
B) My name is Nari Choi.
A) What's your first name?
B) Nari.
A) What's your last name?
B) Choi.

A) What's your student number?
B) It's 1-2-3-9-8-7-4-5-6.
A) How old are you?
B) I'm 12 years old.

11: b) Listening Comprehension T5

Fill in the missing information by listening to the conversations.

	Peter	Robert
Last Name		
Student Number		
Age		

12: a) Write your own conversation (Introductions)

Write a conversation wherein you introduce two of your friends to one another.

You: ______________________________

Friend 1: ______________________________

Friend 2: ______________________________

Friend 1: ______________________________

Friend 2: ______________________________

Now practice the conversations with your group.

12: b) Write your own conversation (Personal Interests)

Write 3 conversations wherein you ask 3 friends about what they do in their free time.

You: ______________________________

Friend 1: ______________________________

You: ______________________________

Friend 2: ______________________________

You: ______________________________

Friend 3: ______________________________

"What do you do in your free time?"

"I like to travel."

Underwater Fun

13) Puzzle

Complete the puzzle below. Search through Unit 1 for possible solutions.

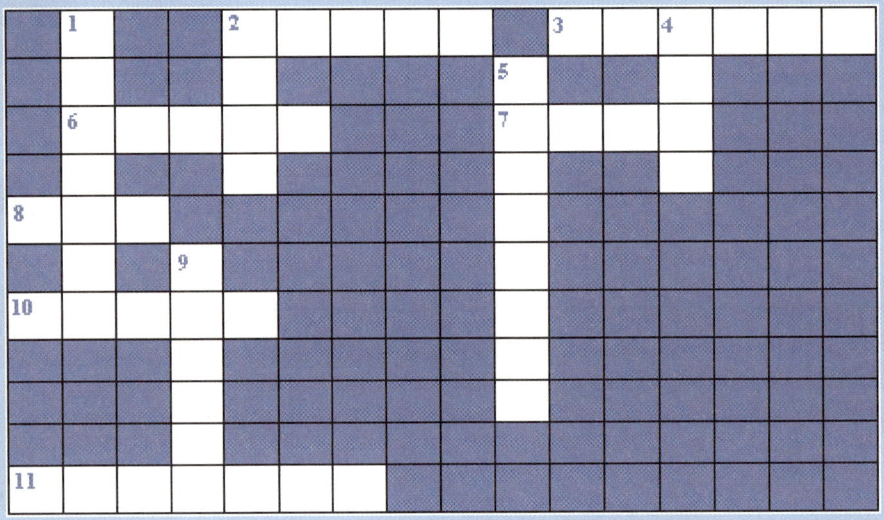

After you have completed the puzzle, check for the solutions at the 'Puzzle Solutions' section at the back of the book.

Across

2) What's your ________ name?
3) Can I have your phone __________?
6) See you _________.
7) I _______ to travel.
8) _______ old are you?
10) I'm 17________ old.
11) What's your __________ number?

Down

1) You're ____________.
2) What do you do in your _________ time?
4) It's good to ________ you.
5) It's a ___________ to meet you.
9) Are you from __________ here?

BUSINESS NAME

Unit 2

Day to Day

During the day

Grammar

Content

- Talking about general routines with the Simple Present

Unit breakdown:

Kinds of Transportation p.16

Ways of getting around p.17

Ways of Acknowledging p.18

Occupations p.19

Occupation Enquiries p.20

Review Activities p.21

Puzzle p.22

The Day is Long

This unit focuses on…

- Kinds of transportation for getting around
- Asking others about the ways they commute
- Asking others about their weekend plans
- Asking people about their occupations

By bus By Train

1) Your Plans

A) What are you doing today?
B) I am visiting my mother.

A) Are you going by bus or train?
B) I think I'm going to take the bus.

A) How long is the trip?
B) It's about 40 minutes.

Now practice the above conversation within your group. Use your own scenarios and say them out loud in English.

---

2) What's your plan?

"What are your plans for tonight?"

A) What are your plans for tonight?
B) I am going to the movies.
A) What are you watching?
B) A romantic comedy.
A) Can I come with you?
B) Sorry. I am going with my girlfriend.

Now practice the above conversation within your group. Use your own scenarios and say them out loud in English. Don't forget to involve all group members.

---

3) Listen to The Conversation T1

- **How are you getting to work today?**
- **By subway.**
- **Is the subway fast?**
- **It's pretty fast.**

4) Are you busy today?

A)

<table>
<tr><td>Are</td><td>you</td><td>getting to</td><td>school</td><td>by</td><td>bus</td><td rowspan="6">?</td></tr>
<tr><td rowspan="2">Is</td><td>Terry</td><td>traveling to</td><td>work</td><td>on the</td><td>subway</td></tr>
<tr><td>your sister</td><td colspan="2">coming</td><td>by</td><td>train</td></tr>
<tr><td>Are</td><td>you</td><td colspan="2">arriving</td><td>on a</td><td>ship</td></tr>
<tr><td>Are</td><td>they</td><td>taking</td><td>a taxi</td><td rowspan="2">to</td><td>work</td></tr>
<tr><td>Is</td><td>the teacher</td><td>riding</td><td>his bicycle</td><td>school</td></tr>
</table>

B)

<table>
<tr><td>Yes,</td><td rowspan="2">I</td><td>think</td><td rowspan="2">so</td><td rowspan="6">.</td></tr>
<tr><td>No,</td><td>don't think</td></tr>
<tr><td colspan="2">I'm</td><td>not</td><td>sure</td></tr>
<tr><td colspan="4">Maybe/Possibly</td></tr>
<tr><td>Yes,</td><td colspan="2">I/he/she/we/they</td><td>am/is/are</td></tr>
<tr><td>No,</td><td colspan="2">I/he/she/we/they</td><td>am not/isn't/aren't</td></tr>
</table>

Now practice the above conversation within your group. Use your own scenarios and say them out loud in English. Don't forget to involve all group members.

5) Listening Activity T2

A) **Mr. Brown. Are you getting to school by car?**

B) **No, I take my scooter.**

A) **Do you commute by scooter every day?**

B) **Only when it's not raining.**

6) On the Weekends

A) **How are you getting to <u>work</u>, <u>Peter</u>?**

B) **I am <u>driving my car</u>.**

A) **Why don't you take <u>the bus</u>?**

B) **It's <u>much faster</u> by <u>car</u>.**

A) **I see.**

Now practice the above conversation within your group. Use your own names while making up your own scenarios and say them out loud in English. Don't forget to involve all group members.

7) Acknowledgements

Now practice the above illustrated ways of greeting and leave-taking. It is important that you know how to use and understand all of them. Don't forget to involve all group members.

8: a) Where are you going? T3

A) Where are you going this weekend?

B) I'm going to the city.

A) Really? Are you taking the bus?

B) No. I am driving my new car.

A) Cool.

Now practice the above conversation within your group. Substitute the underlined information with your own words. Say your conversations out loud in English. Don't forget to involve all group members.

8: b) What do you do? T4

A) What do you do?

B) I am a ticket sales agent.

A) What company do you work for?

B) I work for a tour boat company.

A) How many hours do you work a week?

B) I work 40 hours a week.

Now ask your group members what they do. Use the conversation in activity 8 as a model for your conversations.

9) What do you do for a living?

A) What do you do for a living, Mr. Park?

B) I am the captain of a boat.

A) Really? What kind of a boat?

B) A tour boat actually.

A) Do you like your job?

B) Yes, I do. The job is really demanding and interesting.

Now take the given conversation and model your own conversations on it. Use your own scenarios.

"What do you do for a living?"

10) Fill in the missing information

Example

Name: Yoo Mikyung

Occupation: Student

Place: Seoul Girls' Middle School

Job: Don't like□ Like ■ Love □

Friend

Name: ____________

Occupation ____________

Place: ____________

Job: Don't like□ Like □ Love □

Now take turns filling in the missing information in the spaces provided. Create assumed identities and give your group members your personal data.

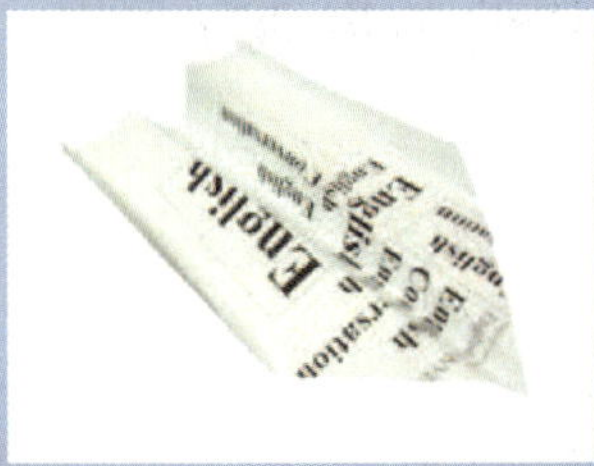

Bridgeways School of English

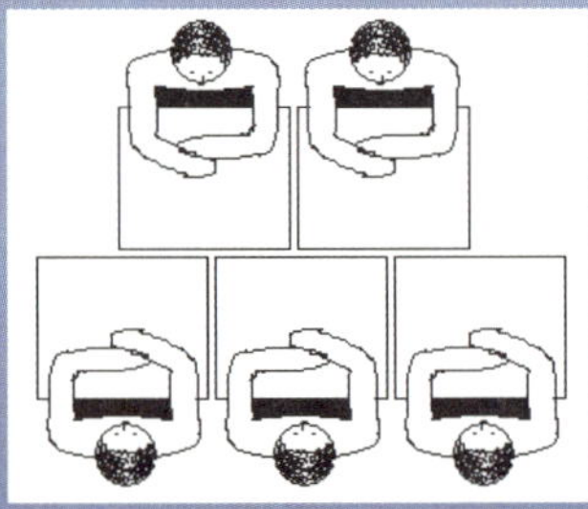

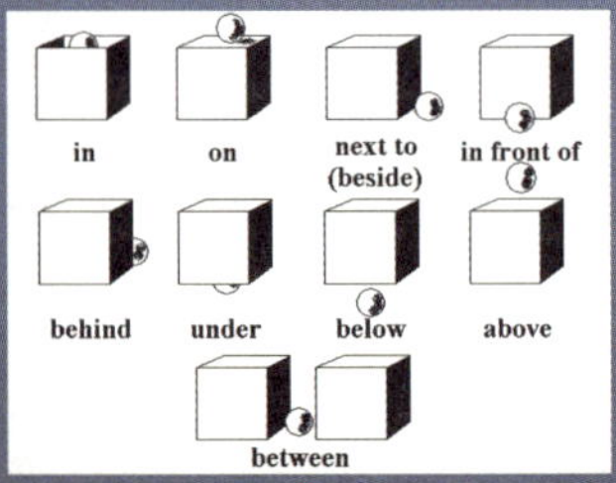

11: a) Fill in the missing information

Fill in the missing information by asking your group members for their personal data.

	Example	Friend1	Friend 2	Friend 3
Name	Go Yuri			
Occupation	Student			
Place of Employment/ Education	Bridgeways School of English			
Number of hours Working/Studying a week	35 hours			
Do you like your job/school?	I love it			

A) What do you do for a living?
B) I am a high school student.

A) Where do you go to school?
B) I attend Bridgeways school of English.

A) How many hours a week do you study?
B) I study 30 hours a week.

A) Do you like your high school?
B) Yes, I love it.

11: b) Listening Comprehension T5

Fill in the missing information by listening to the conversations.

	Margaret	Suzy
Occupation		
Place of Employment/ Education		
Number of Hours Working/ Studying a		

12: a) Write your own conversation (What do you do?)

Write a conversation wherein you ask someone what they do for a living.

A) ____________________

B) ____________________

A) ____________________

B) ____________________

A) ____________________

B) ____________________

A) ____________________

B) ____________________

Now act out the conversations you wrote with your group members. Remember to involve all group members.

12: b) Write your own conversation (Weekends)

Write a conversation wherein you ask someone about what s/he does on the weekends.

A) ____________________

B) ____________________

A) ____________________

B) ____________________

A) ____________________

B) ____________________

A) ____________________

B) ____________________

"What do you usually do on the weekends?"

13) Puzzle

Use the sentences found in Unit 2 to help you complete the following puzzle.

After you have completed the puzzle, check the 'Puzzle Solutions' section at the back of the book for the solution to the above puzzle.

Across

3) How _______ is the trip?

5) How many ________ a week do you study?

7) What are you __________ today?

9) It's much __________ by car.

10) I am _________ my car.

11) Where are you _________ this weekend?

Down

1) What are your _______ for tonight?

2) What __________ do you work for?

4) How are you __________ to work?

6) I ___________ by bus every day.

8) What do you do for a __________?

Unit 3
On the Job

BUSINESS NAME

Grammar

Content

- Expressing the future
- Some proper uses of 'Why?'

Unit breakdown:

Random Questions p.24

I'd like to be a/ an ... p.25

Keeping a conversation p.26

Why do you like your job? p.27

Active Listening p.28

Review Activities p.29

Puzzle p.30

I love my job.

This unit focuses on ...

- Making general enquiries about work and school
- How to express future aspirations
- How to ask for reinforcement (Is that so?/Are you sure?)
- How to bring a conversation to an end

Wow! I'm proud

1) Is your mother a ..?

A) Is your mother a homemaker?
B) No, she's a policewoman.

A) Wow! Does she enjoy her job?
B) Yes, she really loves being a police woman.

A) Are you proud of her?
B) Yes, I am very proud of her.

Now practice the above conversation within your group. Use your own scenarios and say them out loud in English. Don't forget to involve all group members.

2) I'd like to be a ...

"I love to sing to jazz music."

A) What is your dream job?
B) I'd like to be a jazz singer.
A) Are you in a band?
B) Yes, I am.
A) What's the name of your band?
B) The Bass Boys.

Now practice the above conversation within your group. Use your own scenarios and say them out loud in English. Don't forget to involve all group members.

3) Listen to The Conversation T1

- **What does your father do for a living?**
- **He cleans ships.**
- **What kind of ships?**
- **Tall ships.**

4) Grammar in Context

A)

<table>
<tr><td>Is</td><td>your mother</td><td colspan="3">a homemaker</td><td rowspan="4">?</td></tr>
<tr><td rowspan="3">What</td><td>is</td><td>your</td><td colspan="2">dream job</td></tr>
<tr><td>does</td><td>your father</td><td>do</td><td>for a living</td></tr>
<tr><td>do</td><td>you</td><td colspan="2">do</td></tr>
</table>

B)

<table>
<tr><td>Yes</td><td>she</td><td colspan="2">is</td><td rowspan="4">.</td></tr>
<tr><td>I'd</td><td>like to be</td><td colspan="2">a hockey player</td></tr>
<tr><td>He</td><td>is</td><td>a policeman</td><td>for the NYPD</td></tr>
<tr><td>I</td><td>am</td><td>a student</td><td>at Bridgeways School of English</td></tr>
</table>

NYPD = New York City Police Department

Now practice the above conversation within your group. Use your own information to construct your own sentences.

5) Listening Activity T2

A) What company does your father work for?

B) He works for CBC.

A) Is he a reporter or an anchorman?

B) He's a cameraman.

6) I'd like to be a medic.

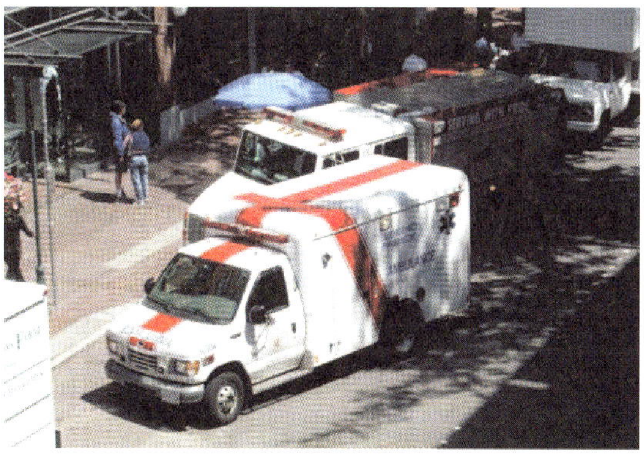

A) What is your dream job?

B) I'd like to be a medic.

A) Do you want to work in a hospital?

B) No. I'd like to be a paramedic in an ambulance.

A) That's nice.

Now practice the above conversation within your group. Use your own information to construct your own sentences.

7) Ways of Continuing Conversations

Now practice the above illustrated ways of continuing conversations. It is important that you know how to use and understand all of them. Don't forget to involve all group members.

8: a) Listening Activity T3

A) I'd like to be a pilot.

B) Are you sure?

A) Yes, I am.

B) Why not a teacher?

A) Because, it's a respected profession and pilots earn much money.

Now practice the above conversation within your group. Use your own scenarios, then say your conversations out loud in English. Don't forget to involve all group members.

8: b) I love the outdoors. T4

A) Why do you like your job?

B) Because I love being out on the sea.

A) No kidding?

B) I hate being indoors all day. I simply love the fresh air and the outdoors.

A) All right.

Ask your group members if they like being students. Use the conversation in activity 8 as a model for your conversations.

9) Why are you a dancer?

A) Why are you a dancer?

B) Because it helps me stay in shape.

A) Are you sure?

B) Yes. Dancing is very good exercise.

A) Oh, I see.

to stay in shape = to keep fit

"Dancing helps me stay in shape."

Now take the conversation and model your own conversations on it. Use your own scenarios.

10) Why do you/don't you like being a student?

Example

Name: David Moore

Being a student: Love □ Like □ Not Like ■ Hate □

Why?/Why not? Because of too much homework

Friend

Name: ______________________

Being a student: Love □ Like □ Not Like □ Hate □

Why?/Why not? ______________________

Now take turns filling in the missing information in the spaces provided.

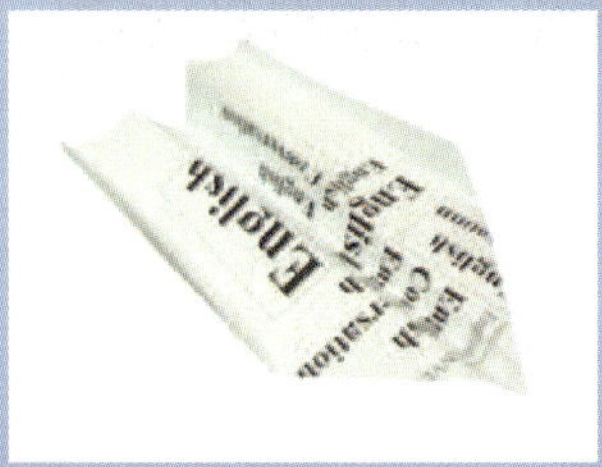

11: a) Fill in the missing information

Fill in the missing information by asking your group members for their personal data.

	Example	Friend1	Friend 2	Friend 3
Name	Nancy Gill			
Do you like your job/school?	Yes I do			
Why do you like your job/school?	Because I like my teacher.			
What is your dream job?	I'd like to be a pilot.			
What does your father do?	He's a policeman.			

A) Do you like your school?
B) Sure I do.

A) Why do you like your school?
B) Because I have a very good teacher.

A) What is your dream job?
B) I'd like to be a pilot because I love flying.

A) What does your father do for a living?
B) My father is a policeman for the NYPD.

11: b) Listening Comprehension T5

Fill in the missing information by listening to the conversations.

	Homer	Tony
Does he like school/work?		
Why does he like school/ work?		
What's his dream job?		

12: a) Write your own conversation (Why is … interesting?)

Write a conversation wherein you ask someone about what s/he finds interesting about her/his job/school.

A) ____________________

B) ____________________

A) ____________________

B) ____________________

A) ____________________

B) ____________________

Now act out the conversations you wrote with your group members. Remember to involve all group members.

12: b) Write your own conversation (What is your dream job?)

Write a conversation wherein you ask someone about their dream job.

A) ____________________

B) ____________________

A) ____________________

B) ____________________

A) ____________________

B) ____________________

A) ____________________

B) ____________________

"What would you like to do for a living?"

13) Puzzle

Use the sentences found in Unit 3 to help you complete the following puzzle.

After you have completed the puzzle, check the 'Puzzle Solutions' section at the back of the book for the solution to the above puzzle.

Across

3) What is your ________ job?
4) Do you want to ________ in a hospital?
5) Is your mother a ________________?
6) Being a ________ is a respected profession.
8) I'd like to be a jazz __________.
10) _____________ I have a very good teacher.
11) No _________?

Down

1) Do you _________ your job?
2) What _________ does your father work for?
3) What ________ your father do for a living?
7) What's his dream _______?
9) What would you like to do for a ________?

Unit 4

Eating Out

BUSINESS NAME

Grammar

Content

- Adjectives in use
- The preposition 'With'

Unit breakdown:

Agreeing with Others p.32

Making Food Choices p.33

'Agreement ' Expressions p.34

Expressing Regret p.35

Listening Comprehensio p.36

Review Activities p.37

Puzzle p.38

What would you like to order today?

This unit focuses on ...

- Kinds of restaurants
- Types of foods
- Ordering in restaurants
- List of foods available on the menu

OK Then, All right!

1) How about Italian?

A) Let's go to an all you can eat buffet.
B) What kind of food are you thinking of?

A) How about an Italian buffet?
B) That sounds good to me.

A) Good, because I could eat a horse.
B) Me too.

I could eat a horse = I am very hungry

Now practice the above conversation within your group. Use your own scenarios and say them out loud in English. Don't forget to involve all group members.

2) That sounds like a good idea.

"That sounds really good."

A)

What do you think	about	Italian food	?
How		McDonalds	
What		KFC	

B)

That	sounds	like	a good plan	.
	is	a really good idea		
	sounds	really good	to me	

A)

Let's	go	and eat	then	.
OK then.	Let's	get	going	
All right!				

Now practice the above conversation within your group. Use your own scenarios and say them out loud in English. Don't forget to involve all group members.

3) Listen to The Conversation T1

- **How about some lobster?**
- **That's a good idea.**
- **All right then. Let's go and eat.**
- **OK.**

4) What's on the menu?

A)

What's	your	daily special		?
What	do	you	recommend	
What's	good	on this	menu	
Can you	recommend	a good dish		

B)

Today's special	is	meat pie	.
I	recommend	the Canadian salmon	
You should	try	the barbecued pork	
The Hungarian goulash	is	wonderful	

Now practice the above conversation within your group. Use your own scenarios and say them out loud with your group. Remember to include all group members.

5) Listening Activity T2

A) **This is a really nice restaurant.**

B) **Do you really think so?**

A) **Yes. The view is wonderful and the food is delicious.**

B) **I agree.**

6) At The Restaurant

Q **Would you like to order?**

A **Yes, I'd like the roast beef.**

Q **Would you like a drink with that?**

A **Yes, I'd like a club soda.**

Q **All right. Your order should be ready in around 15 minutes.**

A **Thank you.**

Now practice the above conversation within your group. Use your own scenarios and say them out loud in English. Don't forget to involve all group members.

7) Agreeing With Others

Now practice the above illustrated ways of agreeing. It is important that you know how to use and understand all of them. Don't forget to involve all group members.

8: a) Chips are not good for you. T3

A) **<u>Chips</u> are really unhealthy.**

B) **Yes, I think so, too.**

A) **<u>Sodas</u> aren't good, either.**

B) **No, they aren't.**

A) **Yes, but <u>orange juice</u> is not bad.**

Now practice the above conversation within your group. Use your own scenarios. Say your conversations out loud in English. Don't forget to involve all group members.

8: b) I'm sorry, we don't... T4

A) I'd like to order some oven baked sausages.

B) I am sorry, we don't have baked sausages, but we have pan fried sausages.

A) That sounds good. I'd like to order that then.

B) OK. Anything to drink with that?

A) Yes. A glass of cola please.

B) Your order will be ready in 10 minutes.

Now ask your group members what foods they like. Use the conversation in activity 8 as a model for your conversations.

9) I'm really sorry, but...

A) I'd like to order pork with rice.

B) I'm really sorry, but we don't have pork on the menu.

A) I'd like some beef then.

B) What kind of beef would you like?

A) Roast beef please.

B) Sure. Your order is coming right up.

"I'm really sorry, but we don't have pork on the menu."

Now take the conversation and model your own conversations on it. Once again use your own information.

10) Pair Work (Do you have ... on the menu? - I'm sorry but ...)

MENU

Japanese Sushi	Italian Style Pasta	Cooked Lobster
Roast Beef	Barbecued Pork	Oven Baked Sausages
Oven Baked Fish	Korean Kimchi	Barbecued Sausages

One of you look at the menu on this page while the other turns to page 114 and look at the menu in activity A). Take turns asking if certain foods are on the other student's menu.

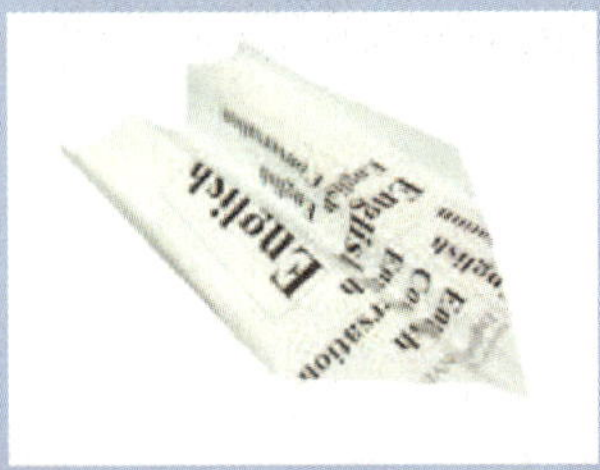

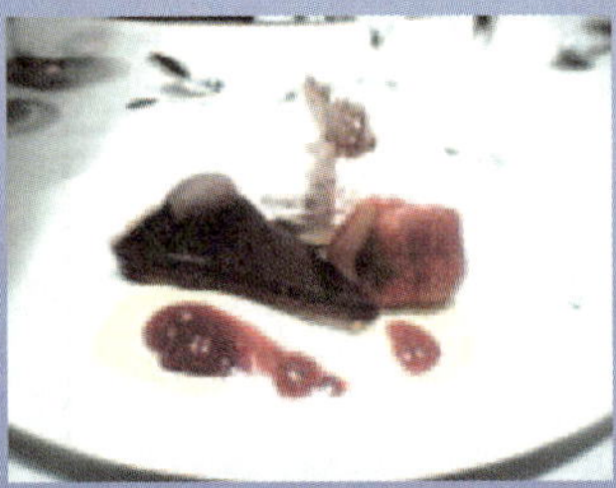

11: a) Fill in the missing information

Fill in the missing information by asking your group members for their answers to the following questions.

	Example	Friend1	Friend 2	Friend 3
Name	Nathan			
What would you like to order?	I'd like the Sweet and Sour Pork.			
What drink would like to order?	I'd like a cup of coffee.			
What do you think about Italian food?	I love Italian food. My favourite food is pizza.			
Would you like to eat at the Outback Steak House?	No thank you. I don't like western food.			

11: b) Listening Comprehension T5

Fill in the missing information by listening to the conversations.

	Brian	Jamie
What restaurant does he go to?		
What would he like to order?		
What does he order?		

12: a) Write your own conversation (What would you like to eat today?)

Write a conversation wherein you ask someone about the kinds of food s/he likes.

A) ______________________________

B) ______________________________

A) ______________________________

B) ______________________________

A) ______________________________

B) ______________________________

A) ______________________________

B) ______________________________

Now act out the conversations you wrote with your group members. Remember to involve all group members.

12: b) Write your own conversation (I think chips are really unhealthy?)

Write a conversation wherein you have a discussion about healthy and unhealthy drinks and foods.

"I really think drinking soda is very unhealthy."

A) ______________________________

B) ______________________________

A) ______________________________

B) ______________________________

A) ______________________________

B) ______________________________

A) ______________________________

B) ______________________________

13) Puzzle

Use the sentences found in Unit 4 to help you complete the following puzzle.

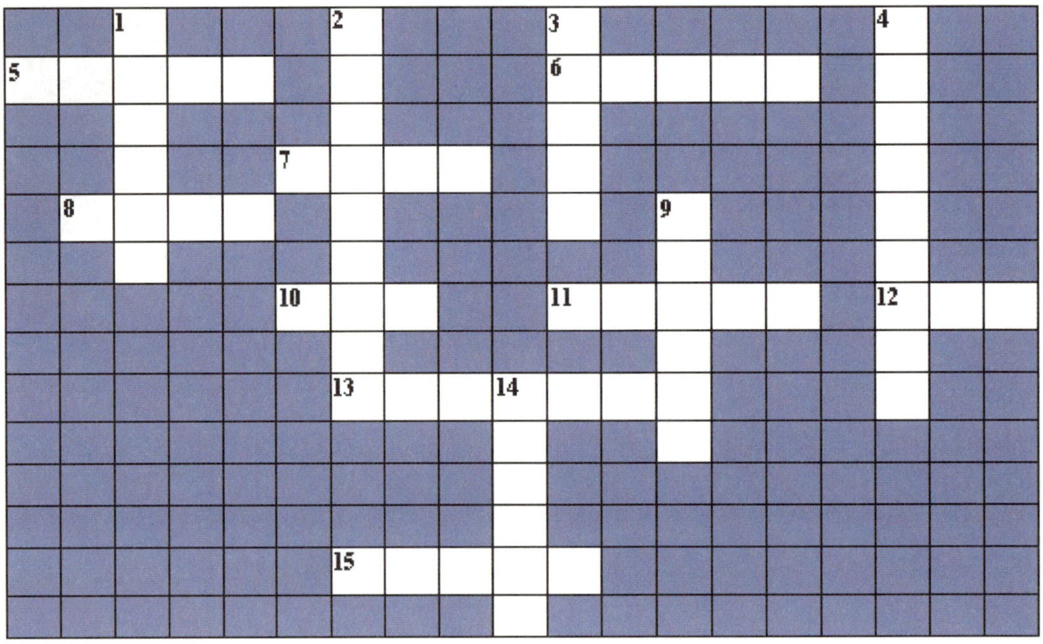

After you have completed the puzzle, check the 'Puzzle Solutions' section at the back of the book for the solution to the above puzzle.

Across

5) What do you think ________ Italian food?

6) I'd like to ________ some Roast Beef.

7) Would you like a drink _______ that?

8) That's a good ________.

10) _______ about an Italian buffet?

11) Your order should be _______ soon.

12) Why don't you _______ the barbecued pork?

13) What's your daily _______?

15) I _______ so too.

Down

1) That _________ like a good plan.

2) The food is very _____________.

3) What kind of beef ________ you like?

4) Chips are really _____________.

9) Do you _________ think so?

14) Your order is _________ right up.

BUSINESS NAME

Unit 5

Money

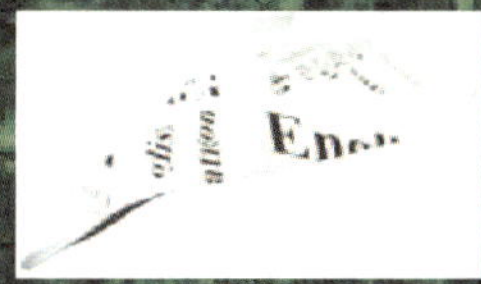

Grammar Content

- Past Tense Questions
- The preposition 'For'

Unit breakdown:

Asking for Change	p. 40
Making Requests	p. 41
Money Terms	p. 42
Denominations	p. 43
Listening Activities	p. 44
Review Activities	p. 45
Puzzle	p. 46

Units of Currency

This unit focuses on ...

- Units of currency
- Asking for change
- Borrowing money
- Asking others to make a purchase
- Learning money related terms

Change Coins

1) Do you have any change?

A) Do you have any change for the bus?
B) How much do you need?

A) I need 800 Won.
B) Sorry, I only have 1,000.

A) A thousand is fine.
B) OK. Here you are.

A) Thank you so much.
B) You're welcome.

Change = Coins or Small Bills

Now practice the above conversation within your group. Use your own scenarios and say them out loud in English. Don't forget to involve all group members.

"Can you give me change for 5,000 won?"

2) How would you like it?

A) Can you give me change for 10,000 won?
B) Yes. How would you like it?
A) Thousand won bills and some coins please.
B) All right. Nine one thousand won bills and some change.

A) Change?
B) Yes, you know? Coins.
A) Oh, I see. Thank you so much.
B) You're welcome.
A) See you later, Mr. Brown.
B) Take care, Jordan.

Now practice the above conversation within your group. Use your own scenarios and say them out loud in English. Don't forget to involve all group members.

3) Listen to The Conversation T1

- Did you lose your wallet?
- No, I didn't.
- Then whose wallet is this?
- I have no idea.

4) Will you buy this purse? T2

A) Will you buy me this purse?

B) How much is it?

A) It's ten dollars and ninety nine cents.

B) That's pretty cheap.

A) Yes, it is. So, will you buy it for me?

B) Of course I will.

A) Thank you, Pete.

B) Sure. It's not a problem, Janet.

Now practice the above conversation within your group. Use your own scenarios and say them out loud in English. Don't forget to involve all group members.

5) Listening Comprehension

		True	False
1)	Janet buys Peter a new purse.	□	□
2)	Peter thinks the purse is expensive.	□	□
3)	Peter does not want to buy the purse.	□	□
4)	Peter thinks the purse is cheap.	□	□
5)	Janet asks Peter for one hundred dollars.	□	□
6)	Janet wants to buy a hand bag, too.	□	□
7)	Peter tells Janet he'll give her ten dollars.	□	□

6) I'd like to borrow some money.

Q **I'd like to borrow 3,000 won.**

A **Sorry. I only have 2,000 and some change.**

Q **That's all right. I just need money for the subway.**

A **OK. Here you are.**

Now practice the above conversation within your group. Use your own scenarios and say them out loud in English. Don't forget to involve all group members.

7) Money Terms

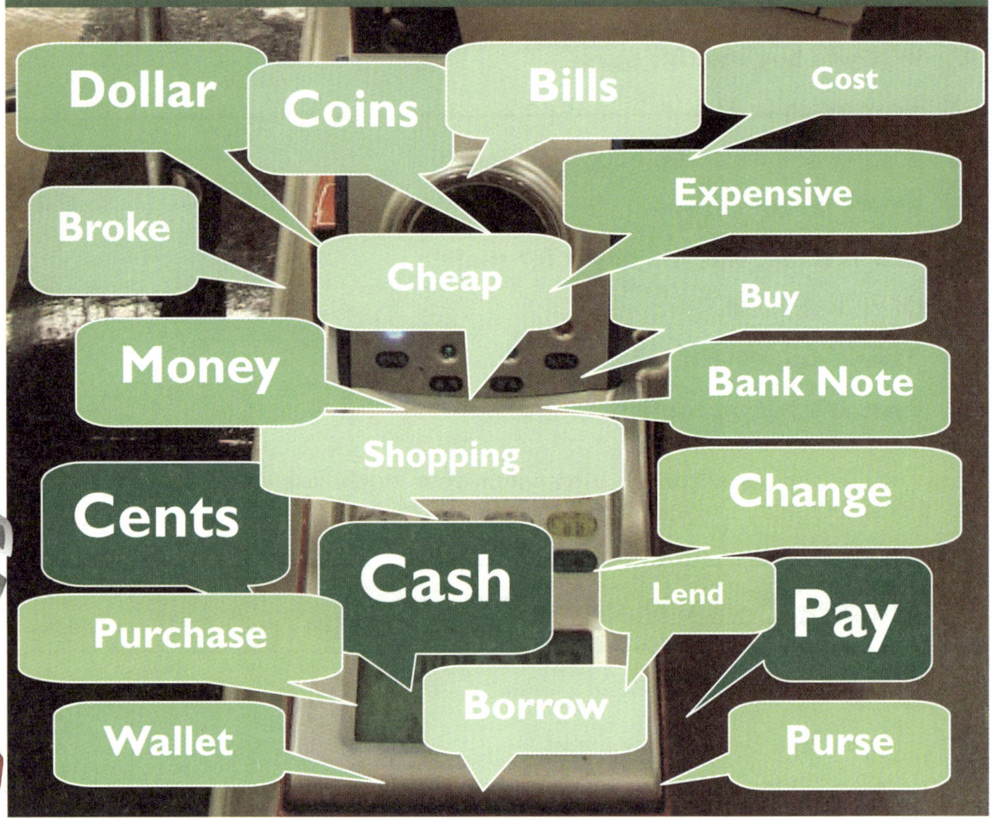

Bills = Paper Bank Notes (Paper Money)
Bills are also things like utility bills such as electricity bills

Now practice the above vocabulary. It is important that you know how to use and understand all of them. Don't forget to involve all group members.

8: a) Breaking Open the Piggy Bank T3

A) Can you break the piggy bank?

B) Don't you have any money?

A) No, I don't. I am broke.

B) Do you have much cash inside?

A) Just a few thousand won.

Now practice the above conversation within your group. Use your own scenarios and say them out loud in English. Don't forget to involve all group members.

8: b) It costs 500 won. T4

A) How much is a pack of gum?

B) It's 500 won.

A) Can you buy it for me?

B) No. Why don't you buy it yourself?

A) Because I am broke.

B) That's too bad.

Model your conversations on the conversation in activity 8.

9) Can you lend me some cash?

A) Can you lend me some money?

B) What for?

A) To purchase that hand bag.

B) That one?

A) No. The one over there.

B) I don't think so.

Now take the given conversation and model your own conversations on it. Once again use your own scenarios.

Lending Some Cash for a Purchase

10) Fill in the missing information

How much money can you lend me?	How much money can you lend me?
I can lend you 25 dollars.	
Will you give it to me in bills and coins?	Will you give it to me in bills and coins?
Two ten dollar bills and a five dollar bill.	

Now take turns asking others to lend you money.

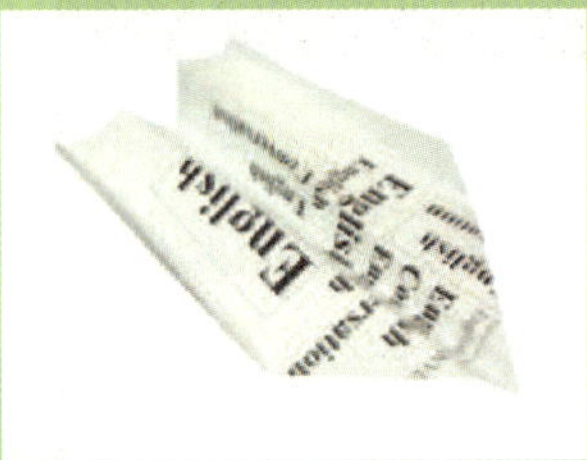

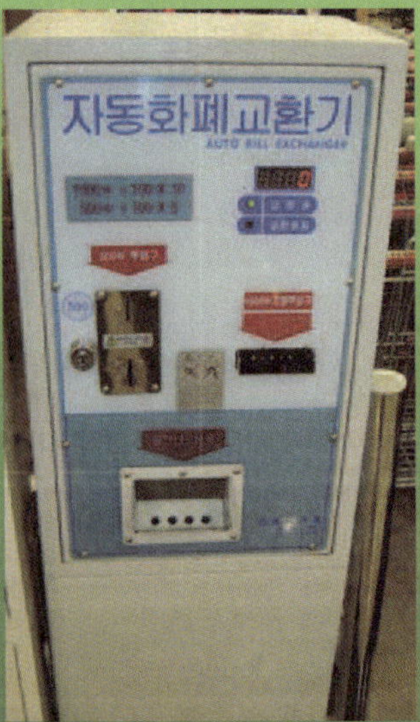

11: a) Fill in the missing information

Fill in the missing information by asking your group members some questions.

	Example	Friend 1	Friend 2
What's your name?	Jung-do		
Do you have any money?	Yes, I do.		
How much do you have?	3,400 won		
Is that in coins or bills?	Three 1,000 won bills and four 100 won coins.		
Can you lend me 1,000 won?	Sorry.		

A) Do you have any money?
B) Yes, I do.

A) How much money do you have on you?
B) 15,000 won.

A) Is that all in one thousand won bills?
B) No. Ten thousand and five thousand.

A) Will you lend me five thousand?
B) Sorry. I need the money for myself.

11: b) Listening Comprehension T5

Fill in the missing information by listening to the conversations.

	Bob	Jerry
How much money does he have?		
How many bills and coins does he have?		
Is he willing to lend any money ?		

12: a) Write your own conversation (Bills and Coins)

Write about asking someone how much money s/he has and whether it's in bills or in coins.

A) ____________________

B) ____________________

A) ____________________

B) ____________________

A) ____________________

B) ____________________

A) ____________________

B) ____________________

Now act out the conversations you wrote with your group members. Remember to involve all group members.

12: b) Write your own conversation (Will you buy me a ..?)

Write a conversation wherein you ask someone to purchase something for you, then act it out with your group.

A) ____________________

B) ____________________

A) ____________________

B) ____________________

A) ____________________

B) ____________________

"Mom! Could you buy me a new car?"

12: c) Borrowing Money

Write about asking someone to lend you some money. (Can I borrow some..?)

____

____

____

____

____

____

____

13) Puzzle

Use the sentences found in Unit 5 to help you complete the following puzzle.

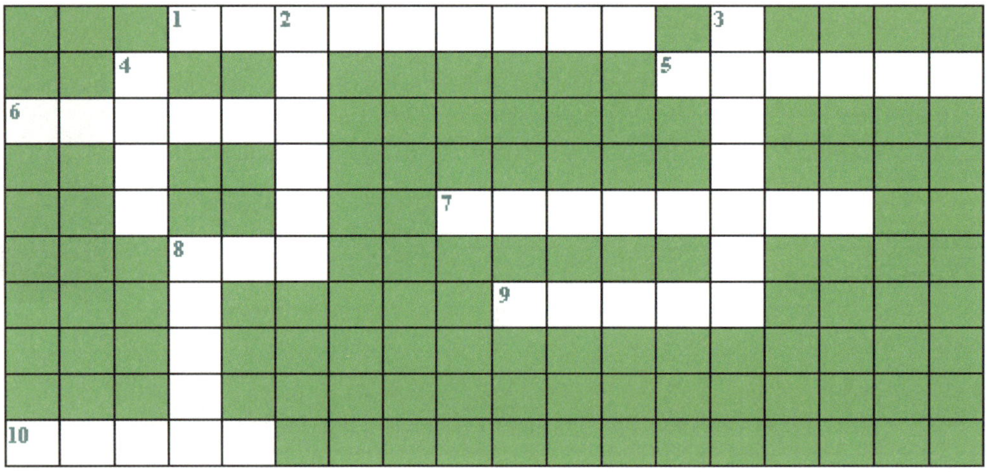

After you have completed the puzzle, check the 'Puzzle Solutions' section at the back of the book for the solution to the above puzzle.

Across

1) John thinks the purse is ________.
5) Can I __________ 100 dollars?
6) Do you have any _______ for the bus?
7) I'd like to ____________ that hand bag.
8) Will you ________ this bag for me?
9) I have five 1,000 won ________.
10) How much _________ do you have?

Down

2) That's ________ cheap.
3) I only have 100 __________.
4) Piggy _________
5) I am _________.

BUSINESS NAME

Unit 6

Traveling & Getting Around

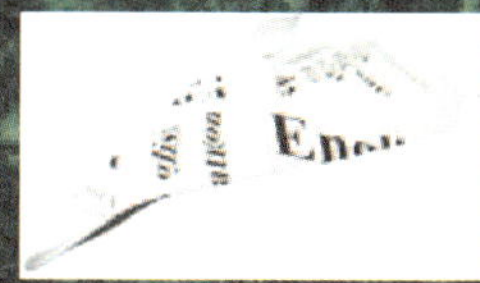

Grammar

Content

- Comparative Adjectives
- Adverbs
- The Modal Verb 'Would'

Unit breakdown:

Taking The Ferry	**p. 48**
Comprehension	**p. 49**
Travel Terminology	**p. 50**
Travel Destinations	**p. 51**
Comprehension Activities	**p. 52**
Review Activities	**p. 53**
Puzzle	**p. 54**

Getting To Your Destination

This unit focuses on …

- Transportation Terminology
- Asking people about their travel plans
- How to offer suggestions
- Modes of transportation

Ferry Ship

1) Let's take the ferry

A) Let's take the ferry.
B) Where to?

A) Let's go to Namba Island.
B) That's a long trip. It's pretty far.

A) Not really. It only takes 45 minutes.
B) Really? Is that all?

A) Yes. The ferry is pretty fast these days.
B) OK. Let's go then.

these days = nowadays

Now practice the above conversation within your group. Use your own scenarios and say them out loud in English. Don't forget to involve all group members.

"Where would you like to go this weekend?"

2) Where would you like to go?

A) Where would you like to go this weekend?

B) Let's go to Bomi Island.

A) Do you want to fly or would you rather take the ferry?

B) I think it's better to take the ferry. It's less expensive.

A) Yes, but it is much slower.

B) That's all right. We have lots of time.

A) That's true. When should we leave then?

B) Let's leave Saturday morning.

A) Sounds good.

Now practice the above conversation within your group. Use your own scenarios and say them out loud in English. Don't forget to involve all group members.

3) Listen to The Conversation T1

- Why don't we take a cruise to the Canary Islands?
- For how long?
- Why don't we go for two weeks?
- That sounds like an excellent idea.

4) I'd like to go by motorcycle. T2

A) Nancy. Would you like to go to the beach?

B) I don't know Nick. I don't really want to go by bus.

A) I don't want to go by bus either. I'd like to go by motorcycle.

B) Isn't that dangerous?

A) No. Not at all. I am very careful you know.

B) I guess. OK, let's go.

A) Hop on then.

B) All right.

hop on = get on

Now practice the above conversation within your group. Use your own scenarios and say them out loud in English. Don't forget to involve all group members.

5) Comprehension Activity

		True	False
1)	Nick wants to go to the beach by bus.	□	□
2)	Nick wants to go to the beach by motorcycle.	□	□
3)	Nancy thinks motorcycles are dangerous.	□	□
4)	Nick thinks motorcycles are dangerous, too.	□	□
5)	Nick is careful when riding his motorcycle.	□	□
6)	Nancy does not go to the beach with Nick.	□	□

6) Walking is good exercise.

Q Would you like to go to <u>the movies</u> with me?

A What's playing?

Q <u>Spiderman 3.</u>

A Really! I love <u>Spiderman</u>.

Q Let's walk there.

A Are you serious?

Q Sure, I am.

Now practice the above conversation within your group. Use your own scenarios and say them out loud in English. Don't forget to involve all group members.

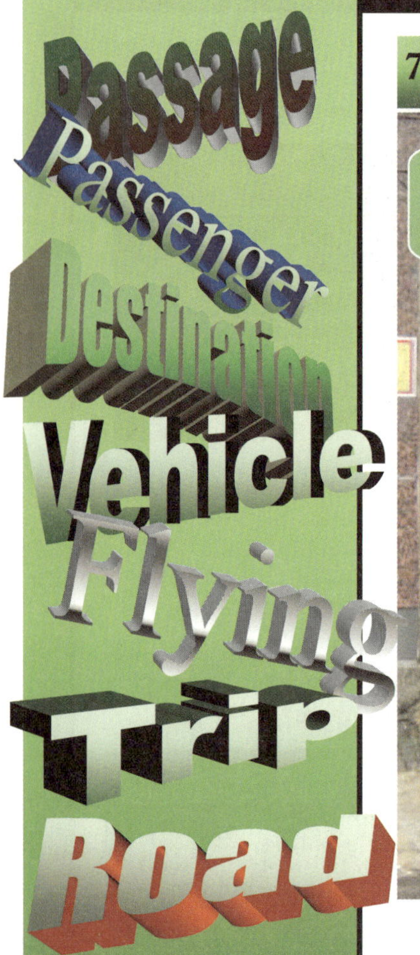

7) Terminology for Getting Around

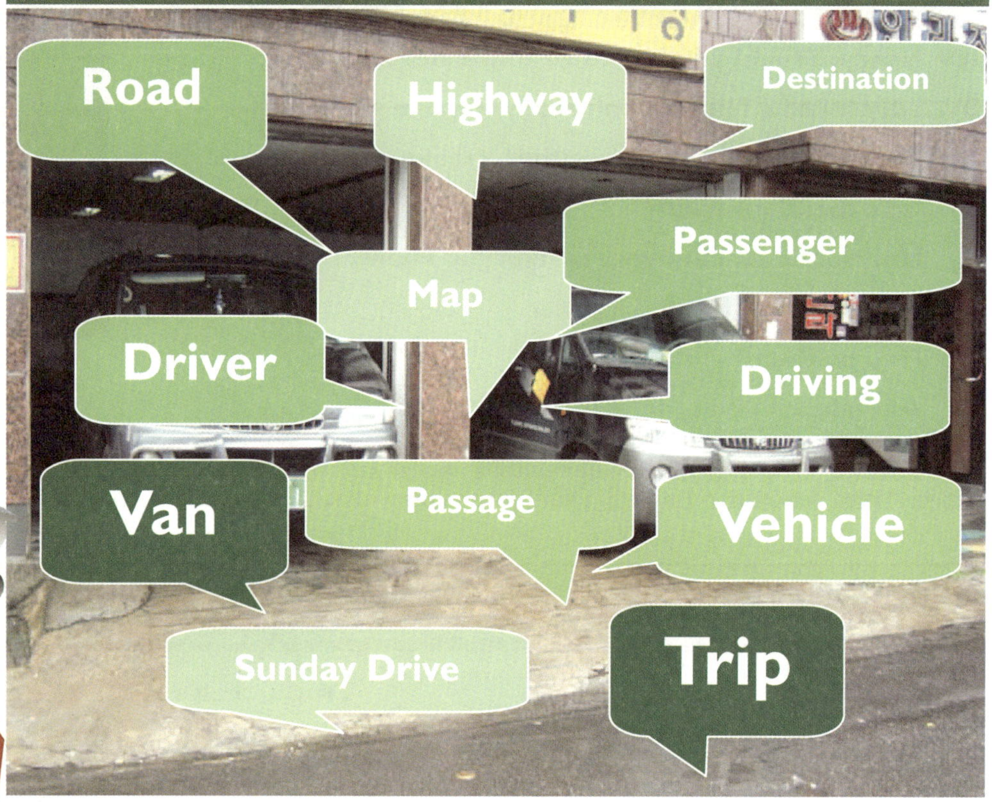

Now practice the above illustrated travel terminology. It is important that you know how to use and understand all of them. Don't forget to involve all group members.

8: a) Going for a Drive T3

A) I am driving to Seoul today.

B) Why don't you take the train?

A) The train is very slow.

B) But it's cheaper to take the train.

A) Yes, but going by car is more comfortable.

B) Do you really think so?

A) Yes. It's also more convenient.

B) All right. It's all the same to me.

A) Well, I'll see you later.

B) Bye now.

Now practice the above conversation within your group. Use your own scenarios and say them out loud in English. Don't forget to involve all group members.

8: b) Have a safe trip. T4

A) What is your destination today?

B) I am going to Tokyo.

A) How are you getting there?

B) I am going by car.

A) Are you driving or will you be a passenger?

B) I'm driving.

A) Are you taking the highway?

B) Yes, I am. It's faster than the roads.

A) Have a safe trip then.

Use the conversation in activity 8 as a model for your conversations.

9) Let's go on a trip to the Philippines.

A) Let's fly to the Philippines.

B) Isn't that too expensive?

A) No. Not at all.

B) OK. When do you want to go then?

A) Why don't we go next week?

B) That's a good idea.

"Let's take a trip to the Philippines."

Now take the given conversation and model your own conversations on it. Once again use your own information.

10) Fill in the missing information

Example	Friend
Where would you like to go?	Where would you like to go?
Los Angeles	
How would you like to get there?	How would you like to get there?
By airplane	
How long would you like to stay?	How long would you like to stay?
Two weeks	

Now take turns filling in the missing information by asking your friends the above questions.

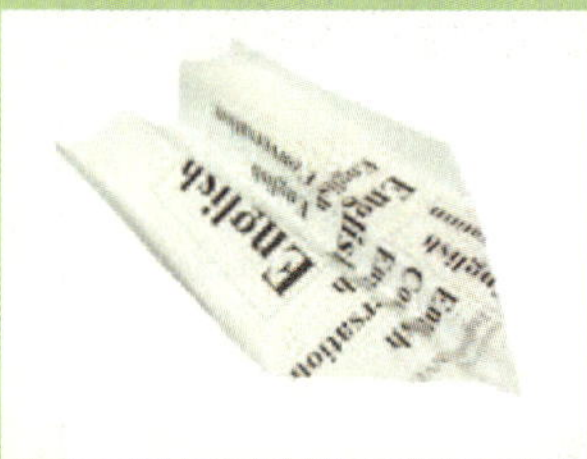

11: a) Fill in the missing information

Fill in the missing information by asking your friends some questions.

	Example	Friend 1	Friend 2	Friend 3
Name	Jason Soars			
Destination	Hawaii			
Mode of Travel	Air			
# of Days	14 days			
# of Passengers	One			

A) Good day Mr. Soars. What is your travel destination today?
B) Honolulu, Hawaii, USA.

A) How are you getting there?
B) I'm flying.

A) How long will you be staying?
B) I'll be staying for 2 weeks.

A) How many members are in your party?
B) I am travelling alone.

11: b) Listening Comprehension T5

Fill in the missing information by listening to the conversations.

	Roger	Rafael
What's his destination?		
How long is he staying?		
How is he getting there?		

12: a) Write your own conversation (Travel Plans)

Write a conversation wherein you ask someone about her/his travel plans.

A) ______________________________

B) ______________________________

A) ______________________________

B) ______________________________

A) ______________________________

B) ______________________________

A) ______________________________

B) ______________________________

Now act out the conversations you wrote with your group members.

12: b) Write your own conversation (Would you like to ..?)

Write a conversation wherein you ask someone if s/he would like to join you on a trip you have planned.

A) ______________________________

B) ______________________________

A) ______________________________

B) ______________________________

A) ______________________________

B) ______________________________

"Would you like to go to the Philippines?"

12: c) Your Next Vacation Plans

Write about your next vacation plans.

____

____

____

____

____

____

____

13) Puzzle

Use the sentences found in Unit 6 to help you complete the following puzzle.

After you have completed the puzzle, check the 'Puzzle Solutions' section at the back of the book for the solution to the above puzzle.

Across

2) I'd like to go _____ bus.

3) _____ on then.

6) Where _______ you like to go?

7) It only _______ 45 minutes to get there.

8) Riding a motorcycle is _______________.

9) It's ____________ to go by train.

10) Are you ______________ alone?

11) How long will you be ____________?

13) That's too ______________.

14) What's your _______________?

Down

1) The ferry is pretty ________ these days.

4) Driving by car is more _____________.

5) It's ___________ to take the ferry.

12) How are you ____________ there?

Unit 7
High-Tech Gadgets

BUSINESS NAME

Grammar

Content

- The Conjunction 'But'
- The Adverb 'Too'

Unit breakdown:

Entertainment Systems p. 56

Can you use a/an ..? p. 57

High-Tech Terminology p. 58

Could I use your ..? p. 59

Comprehension Activities p. 60

Review Activities p. 61

Puzzle p. 62

High-Tech Devices

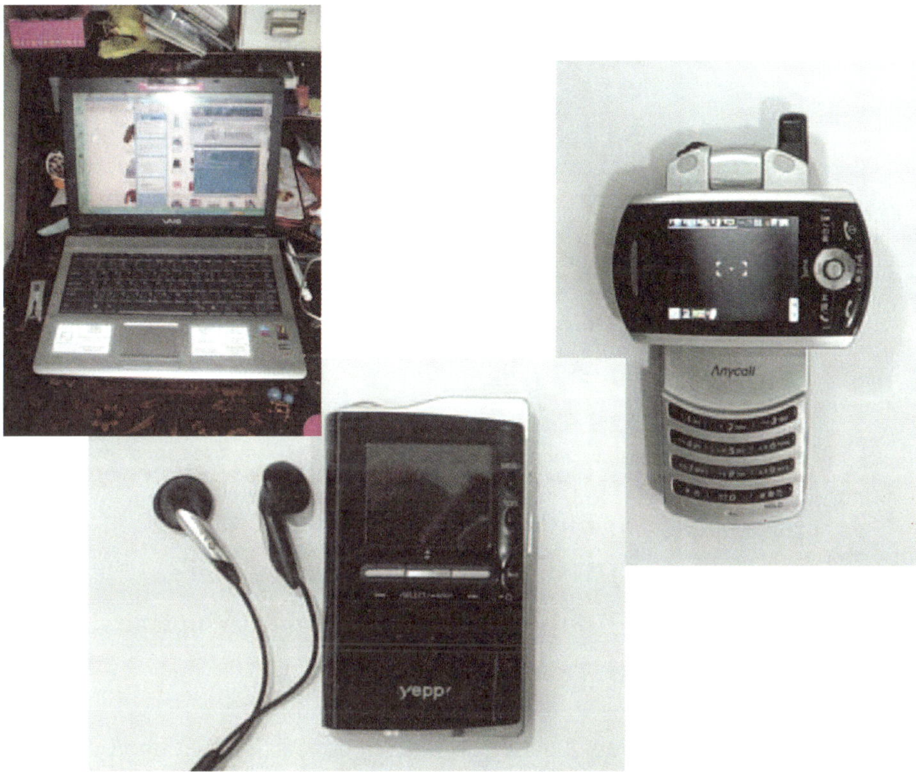

This unit focuses on …

- High-Tech Terminology
- Asking people whether they can use a certain High-Tech device
- Asking for permission to use other people's High-Tech gadgets
- High-Tech device usages and functions

High Definition

1) HD (High Definition) TVs

A) I bought a new high definition TV.
B) Really? HD TVs are the best.

A) Yes. The picture quality is very good.
B) How much did you pay for it?

A) It cost a lot of money.
B) I would like to buy one as well.

HD = High Definition
as well = too

Now practice the above conversation within your group. Use your own scenarios and say them out loud in English. Don't forget to involve all group members.

"That's too bad."

2) Remote Controls

A) Could you please hand me the remote controller?
B) Why?
A) I would like to change the channel.
B) No. I am watching this show. It's very interesting.
A) But, the football game is on.
B) Go upstairs and watch TV there.
A) But mom is watching the TV upstairs.
B) That's too bad.

hand me = give me

Now practice the above conversation within your group. Use your own scenarios and say them out loud in English. Don't forget to involve all group members.

3) Listen to the Conversation T1

- **Can you turn down the volume?**
- **Why?**
- **I can't hear myself, I think.**
- **All right, dad.**

4) Can you use a computer? 🎧 T2

A) **Sue. Can you use a computer?**

B) **Sure Kevin. It's easy.**

A) **Can you teach me how?**

B) **Yeah. Why not?**

A) **Do you know how to send e-mail?**

B) **Yes. That's easy too.**

A) **Do you play computer games on your computer?**

B) **All the time.**

Now practice the above conversation within your group. Use your scenarios and say them out loud in English. Don't forget to involve all group members.

---

5) Comprehension Activity

		True	False
1)	Kevin knows how to use a computer.	☐	☐
2)	Sue knows how to use a computer well.	☐	☐
3)	Kevin does not want to teach Sue how to use a computer.	☐	☐
4)	Kevin doesn't know how to send e-mail.	☐	☐
5)	Kevin does know how to send e-mail.	☐	☐
6)	Kevin never plays computer games.	☐	☐

---

6) I'd like a projector as well.

Q **Wow! You have a large screen TV.**

A **The screen is big, but it's not a TV.**

Q **What is it then?**

A **It's a projector.**

Q **Awesome. I'd like to buy one as well.**

A **Sure. Why not?**

Now practice the above conversation within your group. Use your own scenarios and say them out loud in English. Don't forget to involve all group members.

7) High-Tech Terminology

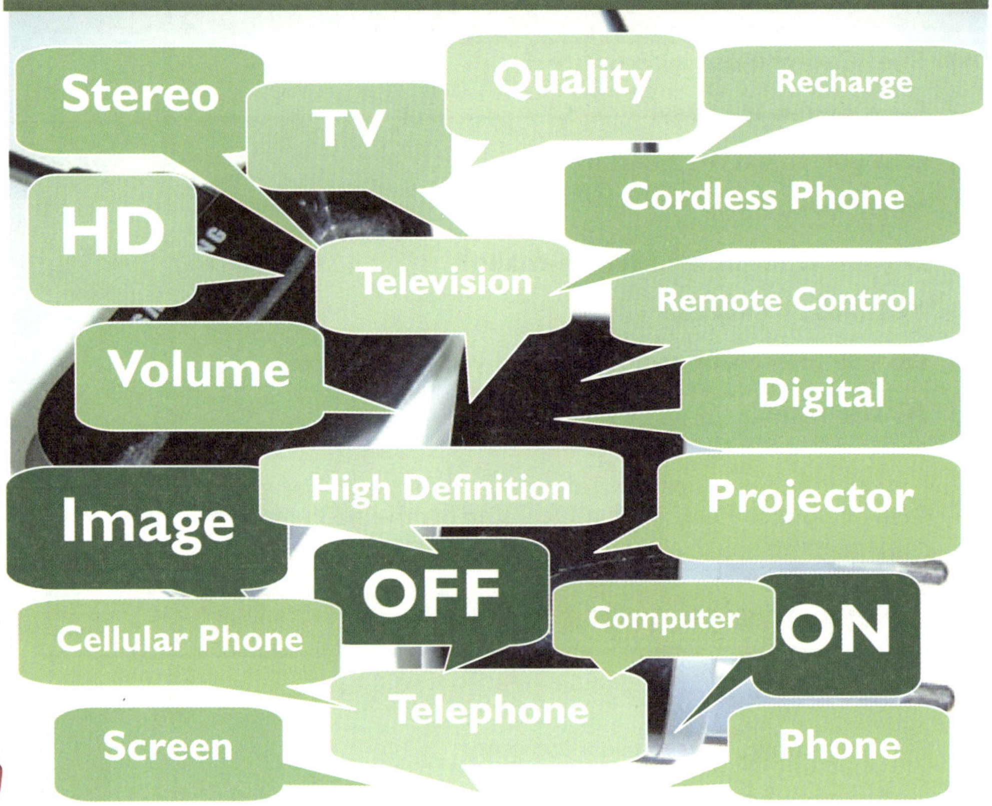

Now practice the above illustrated terminology. It is important that you know how to use and understand all of them. Don't forget to involve all group members.

8: a) Listen to the Conversation T3

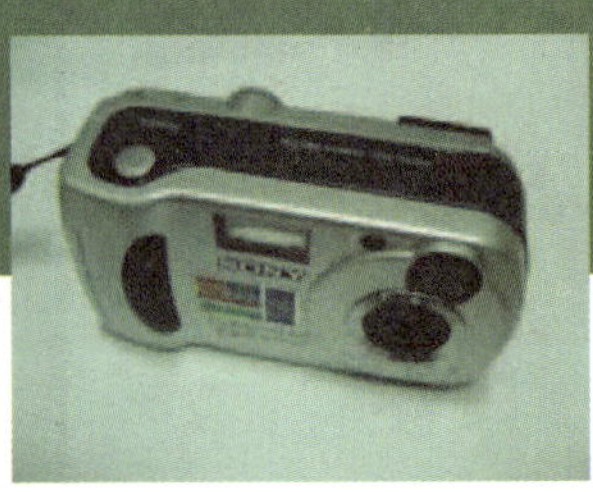

A) I'd like to buy a good quality digital camera.

B) Why don't you buy a SONY camera?

A) Are they any good?

B) Sure. I have 3 Sony cameras. I am very happy with the quality.

A) Where can I buy a SONY camera?

B) Just about anywhere.

A) Really?

B) Yes.

just about = almost

Now practice the above conversation within your group. Use your own scenarios and say them out loud in English. Don't forget to involve all group members.

8: b) Cellular Telephones T4

A) I have a new cell phone I'd like to show you.

B) You mean a cellular telephone?

A) Yes. That is what I mean.

B) It's nice and small.

A) Yes, and I can play games on it too.

B) What games can you play?

A) Racing Time for one.

B) What kind of game is that?

A) It's a car racing game.

B) Nice.

Now use the conversation in activity 8 as a model for your conversations.

9) My Mom's Cordless Phone

A) Could I use your cell phone?

B) Sorry, my battery is low. I need to recharge it, but you can use my mom's cordless phone.

A) Where is it?

B) It's right over there.

A) Thanks.

B) You're welcome.

Now take the given conversation and model your own conversations on it. Once again use your own scenarios.

"I'd like to use your phone."

10) Fill in the missing information

A) Could I use your computer?

B) Sorry, my computer is broken, but you can use the one in the computer room.

A) Where is that?

B) It's over there.

A) Could I use your ____________?

B) Sorry, my __________ is broken, but you can use the one ____________________.

A) Where is that?

B) It's over there.

Now take turns filling in the missing information, then say the conversations aloud with your group.

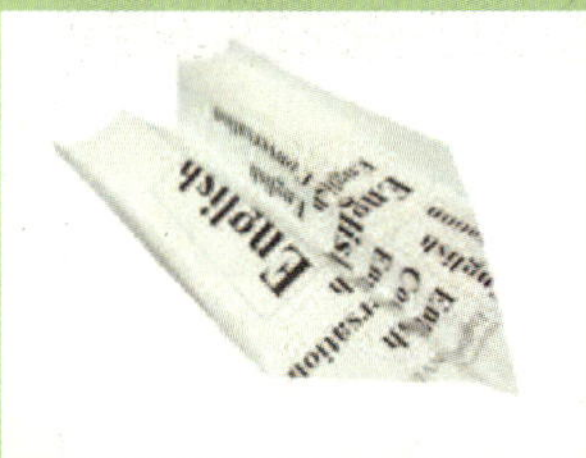

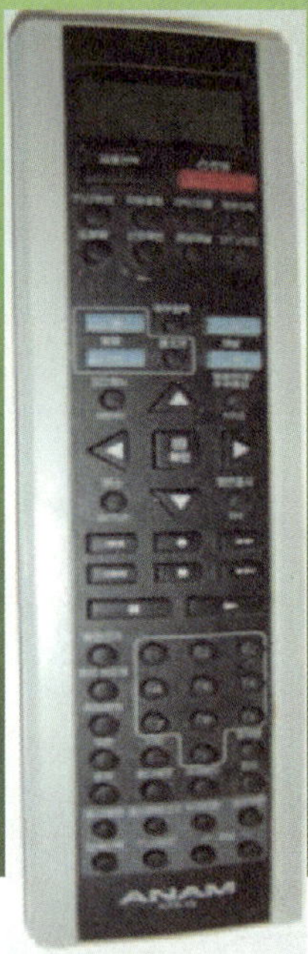

11: a) Fill in the missing information

Fill in the missing information by asking your friends some questions.

	Example	Friend 1	Friend 2	Friend 3
Name	Hyun-sa			
HD TV	Yes			
Cell Phone	Yes			
Computer	No			
Digital Camera	Yes			

A) Do you or your parents own a high definition TV?
B) Yes, we do.

A) Do you or your parents own a cellular telephone?
B) Of course.

A) Do you or your parents own a computer?
B) No, we don't.

A) Do you or your parents own a digital camera?
B) Yes, we do.

11: b) Listening Comprehension T5

Fill in the missing information by listening to the conversations.

	Jeremy	Brad
Does he own an HD TV?		
Does he own a Playstation 3?		
Does he own an XBox?		

12: a) Write your own conversation (Do you own a ..?)

Write about asking someone if s/he owns certain high-tech gadgets.

A) ____________________

B) ____________________

A) ____________________

B) ____________________

A) ____________________

B) ____________________

A) ____________________

B) ____________________

Now act out the conversations you wrote with your group members. Remember to involve all group members.

12: b) Write your own conversation (Could I use your ..?)

Write a conversation wherein you ask someone if you could use one of her/his high-tech gadgets, then act it out with your group.

A) ____________________

B) ____________________

A) ____________________

B) ____________________

A) ____________________

B) ____________________

"May I use your cell phone?"

12: c) Do you know how to use a ..?

Write a conversation wherein you ask someone if s/he knows how to use a certain high-tech gadget.

____

____

____

____

____

____

13) Puzzle

Use the sentences found in Unit 7 to help you complete the following puzzle.

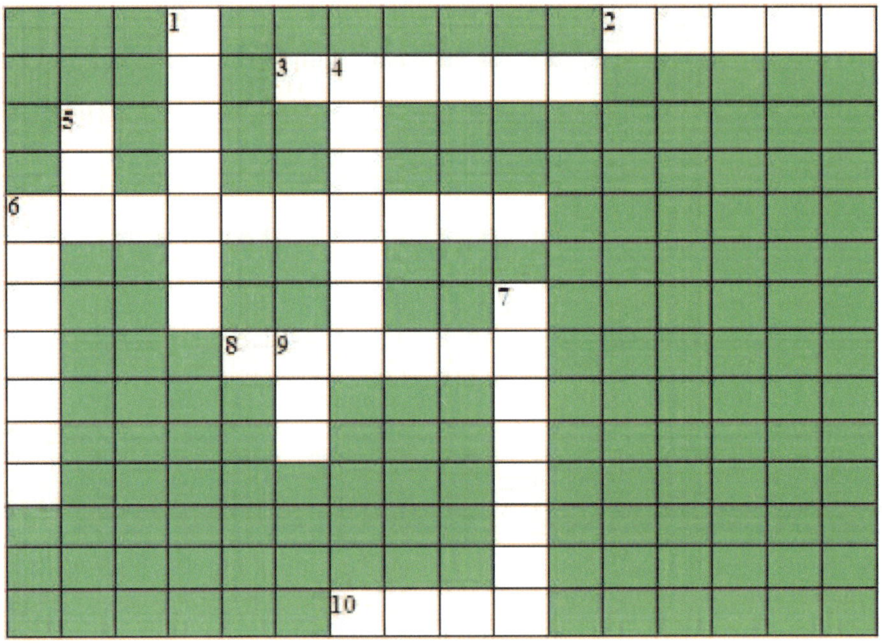

After you have completed the puzzle, check the 'Puzzle Solutions' section at the back of the book for the solution to the above puzzle.

Across

2) Cordless ________.

3) Large ________ TV.

6) High ________

8) Can you turn down the ________?

10) It's right ________ there.

Down

1) The picture ________ is quite good.

4) Could you give me the remote ________?

5) Do you know how to _____ a computer?

6) ________ Camera

7) ________ Telephone

9) Do you ________ an HD TV?

Unit 8
Entertainment

BUSINESS NAME

Grammar

Content

- Casual Language in Real Contexts
- Slang Expressions

Unit breakdown:

Movie Titles & Genres p.64

Video Games & Consoles p.65

Entertainment Terms p.66

Entertainment Choices p.67

Comprehension Activities p.68

Review Activities p.69

Puzzle p.70

I Need Some Entertainment

This unit focuses on …

- Entertainment Terminology
- The kinds of games and consoles
- Movie Genres
- Selecting the right movies

DVDs Videos

1) Movie Genres

A) I'd like to choose a good movie.
B) What kind of movie do you like?

A) I like romantic comedies.
B) Try that section there.

A) The comedy section?
B) Yes. That one.

A) Thank you for your help.
B) It's my pleasure.

It's my pleasure = you're welcome

Now practice the above conversation within your group. Use your own scenarios and say them out loud in English. Don't forget to include all your group members.

"How about an action movie?"

2) Shopping for a Movie

A) Let's buy an action movie.
B) Which one?
A) How about The Dirty Dozen?
B) No. That's way too old.
A) What about Ocean's 13 then?
B) Is that the movie with Brad Pitt in?
A) Yes.
B) I think Brad Pitt is a good actor. It's a good choice.
A) All right. Ocean's 13 is it.

Now practice the above conversation within your group. Use your own scenarios and say them out loud in English. Don't forget to include all group members.

3) Listen to The Conversation T1

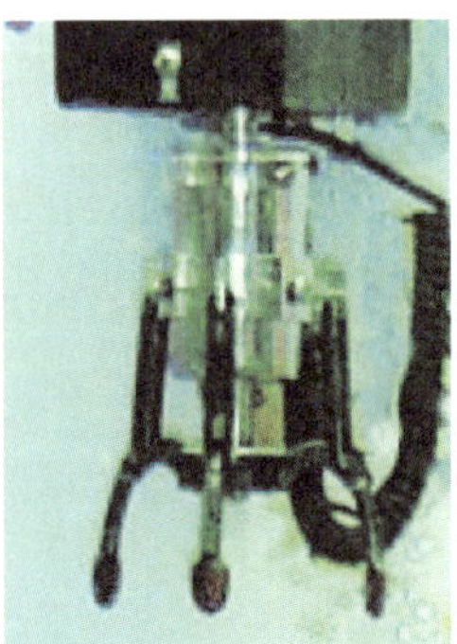

- Hold on. I want to play the crane game.
- What can you win with this game?
- All kinds of stuff. Mostly toys really.
- Cool. Let me give it a go.

4) Playing Video Games T2

A) Mike. Do you want to give this game a go?

B) What game is that, Paul?

A) It's Halo 3. It's a really fantastic game.

B) Would you like to play one on one?

A) You mean you against me?

B) Sure. Why not?

A) OK then. Let's give it a go.

B) I bet I can beat you.

Now practice the above conversation within your group. Use your own scenarios and say them out loud in English. Don't forget to involve all group members.

---

5) Comprehension Activity

		True	False
1)	Mike wants Paul to play Halo 3 with him.	□	□
2)	Paul thinks Halo 3 is childish.	□	□
3)	Paul wants to give it a go.	□	□
4)	Mike wants to play one on one with Paul.	□	□
5)	Paul does not want to play one on one with Mike.	□	□
6)	Mike thinks he can beat Paul.	□	□

---

6) What kind of console do you have?

Q **What kind of console do you have?**

A **I have an XBox 360. How about you?**

Q **I have a Playstation 3.**

A **It's made by SONY, right?**

Q **Yes, it is.**

A **Well. XBox is made by Microsoft.**

Now practice the above conversation within your group. Use your own scenarios and say them out loud in English. Don't forget to involve all group members.

7) Movie Genres and Entertainment Terminology

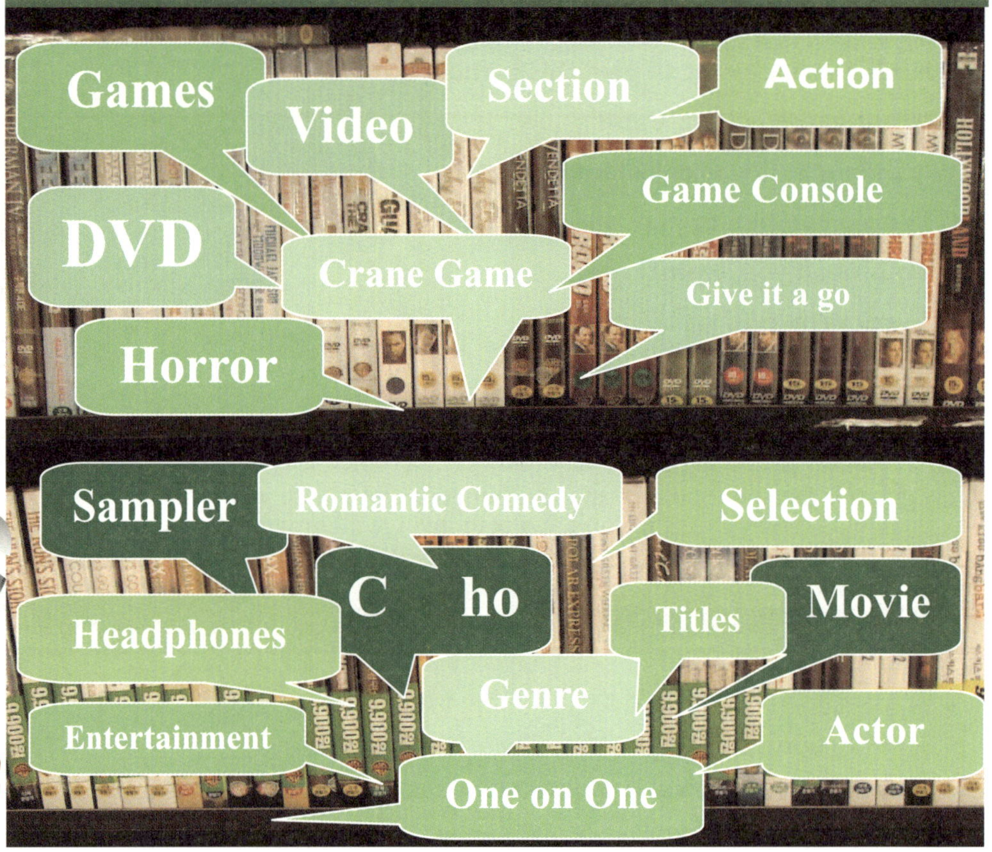

Now practice the above illustrated entertainment terms. It is important that you know how to use and understand all of them. Don't forget to involve all group members.

8: a) Push play when you are ready. 🎧 T3

A) I love <u>Pop</u> music. Can I listen to this one by <u>The Beatles</u>?

B) Sure. The CD sampler is right over there. Just put on the headphones and listen away.

A) Cool.

B) Push play when you are ready.

A) Thanks for the help.

B) I'm glad to be of service.

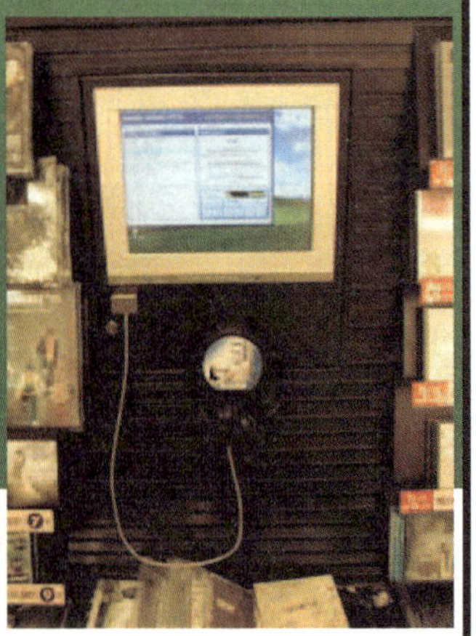

Now practice the above conversation within your group. Use your own scenarios and say them out loud in English. Don't forget to involve all group members.

8: b) This Band is Hot T4

A) This band is hot.

B) Do you know who they are?

A) I don't know, but they play reggae, I think.

B) Are you sure?

A) Yes, I am pretty sure.

B) I think I'm going to like reggae music.

A) Probably.

Use the conversation in activity 8 as a model for your conversations.

---

9) Let's pick a good movie.

A) There is nothing on TV.

B) Let's watch a movie then.

A) Do you have any DVDs?

B) Sure. Just take your pick.

A) All right. I like this one.

B) This is a musical.

A) Yes, I know. I like musicals.

B) OK. Let's watch it.

"There is nothing on TV. Let's watch a movie."

Now take the given conversation and model your own conversations on it. Once again use your own scenarios.

---

10) Fill in the missing information

Example	Friend
What kind of movies do you like?	What kind of movies do you like?
I like horror movies.	
What is your favourite video game?	What is your favourite video game?
I love Halo 3	

Now take turns filling in the missing information by asking your friends some questions.

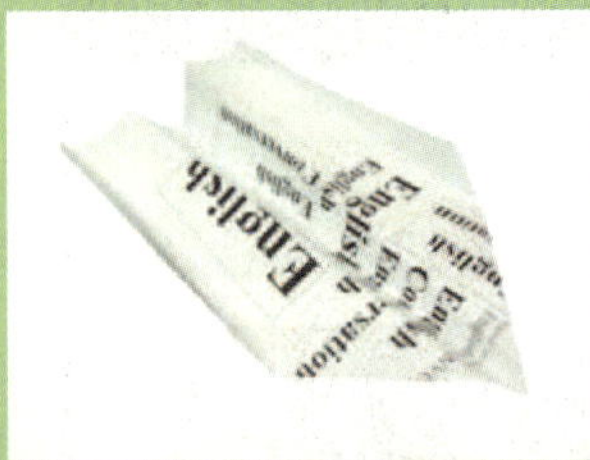

11: a) Fill in the missing information

Fill in the missing information by asking your friends some questions.

	Example	Friend 1	Friend 2	Friend 3
Name	Chris			
Do you like horror movies?	Yes, I do.			
What is your favourite video game?	War Craft			
Did you ever play the crane game?	Of Course.			
What did you win?	I won a teddy bear.			

A) Do you like horror movies?
B) Yes. Horror movies are really good.

A) What did you win on the crane game?
B) I won a teddy bear a long time ago.

11: b) Listening Comprehension T5

Fill in the missing information by listening to the conversations.

	Jackie	Cathy
What kind of movie genre does she like?		
Did she ever play the crane game?		
What did she win on the crane game?		

12: a) Write your own conversation (What kind of ...?)

Write a conversation where you ask someone what kind of movies s/he watches.

A) ______________________________

B) ______________________________

A) ______________________________

B) ______________________________

A) ______________________________

B) ______________________________

A) ______________________________

B) ______________________________

Now act out the conversations you wrote with your group members. Remember to involve all group members.

12: b) Write your own conversation (Do you play ...?)

Write a conversation wherein you ask someone whether s/he plays video games, then act it out with your group.

A) ______________________________

B) ______________________________

A) ______________________________

B) ______________________________

A) ______________________________

B) ______________________________

"Do you like playing video games? What kind of games do you play?"

12: c) Let's buy an action film.

Write a conversation wherein you and your friend go movie shopping.

____

____

____

____

____

____

____

13) Puzzle

Use the sentences found in Unit 8 to help you complete the following puzzle.

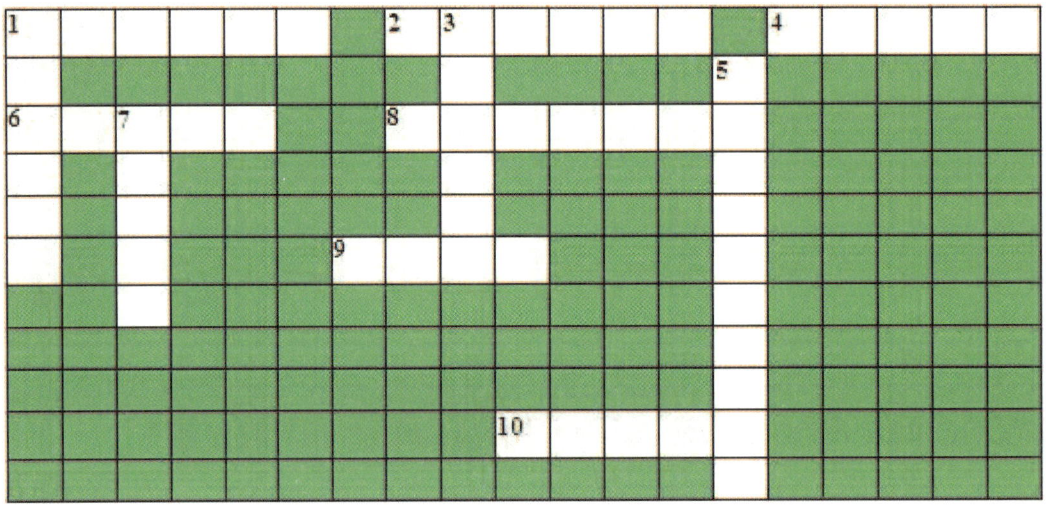

After you have completed the puzzle, check the 'Puzzle Solutions' section at the back of the book for the solution to the above puzzle.

Across

1) I'd like to ________ a good movie.

2) I like __________ movies.

4) I'd like to play the ________ game.

6) Let's watch a _________ then.

8) I have an XBox __________.

9) What about Ocean's 13 ________?

10) What kind of movie ________ do you like?

Down

1) Romantic ___________

3) It's a good ________.

5) Just put on the ______________ and listen away.

7) What's your favorite _________ game?

Unit 9

Daily Exercise

Grammar Content

- The Comparative Phrase 'Better Than ...'
- 'Things like ...' Phrases
- 'I'd Rather ...' Phrases

Unit breakdown:

Hard Work or Fun?	p. 72
Tennis In The Park	p. 73
Exercise Related	p. 74
Building Muscle	p. 75
Comprehension Activities	p. 76
Review Activities	p. 77
Puzzle	p. 78

Things to do to stay in shape

This unit focuses on ...

- Exercise related terminology
- How to express the preference of one thing over another
- Inviting others to do exercise or to partake in sports
- The various kinds of exercise

AB SLIDER

1) Let's work on our abs.

A) Let's work on our abs.
B) How do you want to do it?

A) Let's use the AB Slider.
B) Isn't that difficult to use?

A) No, not at all. It's really easy.
B) But, it's hard work nonetheless.

A) Let's just do it.
B) OK.

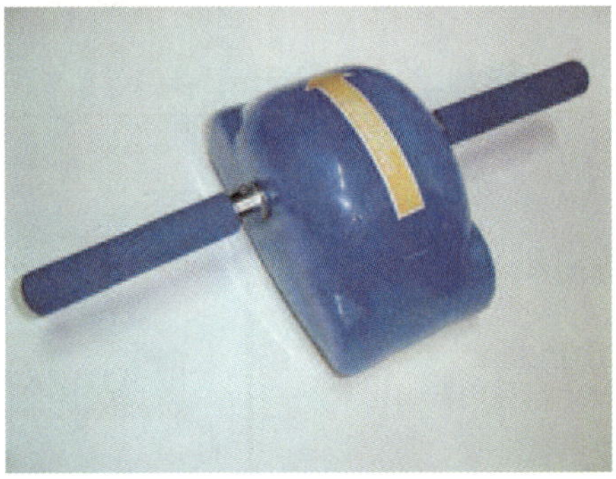

abs = stomach muscles

Now practice the above conversation within your group. Use your own scenarios and say them out loud in English. Don't forget to involve all group members.

"I need some exercise, but I'd like to do something fun."

2) Badminton is fun.

A) I'd like to do some exercise, but I'd like to do something fun.
B) How about badminton?
A) That sounds like a good idea.
B) Let's go to the park to play.
A) Oops! I don't have any rackets.
B) That's all right. I have a pair.
A) Well, what are we waiting for? Let's go then.
B) I'll race you to the park.

Now practice the above conversation within your group. Use your own scenarios and say them out loud in English. Don't forget to include all group members.

---

3) Listen to The Conversation T1

- Table tennis is very popular in China.
- Is it popular in the USA?
- No, not really.
- What's popular in the USA then?
- Basketball and baseball.

4) Playing Tennis T2

A) **Michael. Are you good at tennis?**

B) **I can play a little.**

A) **Are you up for a match then?**

B) **You mean with you?**

A) **Sure. Why not?**

B) **But Benjamin, you play so much better than me.**

A) **Don't worry. I'll take it easy on you.**

B) **I sure hope so.**

Now practice the above conversation within your group. Use your own scenarios and say them out loud in English. Don't forget to involve all group members.

5) Comprehension Activity

		True	False
1)	Michael can play tennis a little.	□	□
2)	Michael plays tennis better than Benjamin.	□	□
3)	Benjamin is a better tennis player than Michael.	□	□
4)	Michael asks Benjamin to play tennis with him.	□	□
5)	Benjamin asks Michael to play tennis with him.	□	□
6)	Benjamin says he will take it easy on Michael.	□	□

"Are you good at tennis?"

"I can play a little."

6) Tennis In The Park

Q **It's a nice day for some to play tennis in the park.**

A **Yes, I agree. Are you up for a game?**

Q **Do you have an extra tennis racket?**

A **Yes, I do.**

Q **Well, let's go then.**

A **Sure. Let's go.**

Now practice the above conversation within your group. Use your own scenarios and say them out loud in English. Don't forget to involve all group members.

7) Exercise-Related Terms

Now practice the above illustrated terms. It is important that you know how to use and understand all of them. Don't forget to involve all group members.

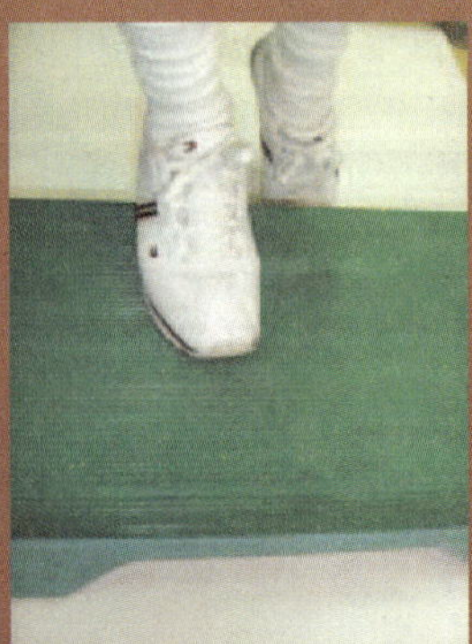

8: a) Aerobics is for everyone. T3

A) Aerobics is good exercise.
B) Yes, it's good cardio.
A) What do you mean by cardio?
B) It's good for the heart.
A) Oh yes, that's so true.
B) It's a good way to break a sweat.
A) How about doing some aerobics together?
B) I don't know. I'd rather do something more fun.
A) Like what?
B) Like playing badminton. Badminton is more fun than aerobics.

Now practice the above conversation within your group. Use your own scenarios and say them out loud in English. Don't forget to involve all group members.

8: b) Dumbbells T4

A) I need to build some muscle.

B) How do you plan on doing that?

A) By going to the gym.

B) What will you do there?

A) I'll lift weights. You know things like dumbbells.

B) Are dumbbells heavy?

A) Some are.

B) I don't like heavy things.

Now ask your group members some questions. Use the conversation in activity 8 as a model for your conversations.

9) Jumping Rope

A) Jumping rope is good cardio exercise.

B) Yes, but it's so boring.

A) Not really.

B) No, thank you. I'd rather play tennis.

A) Do you want to try jumping rope?

B) No, thank you.

A) All right. Suit yourself.

"Suit yourself."

Now take the given conversation and model your own conversations on it. Once again use your own scenarios.

10) Fill in the missing information

What kind of exercise do you like to do?	What kind of exercise do you like to do?
I like doing aerobics.	
What kind of sport do you think is fun?	**What kind of sport do you think is fun?**
I think tennis is really fun.	

Now take turns filling in the missing information by asking your friends some questions.

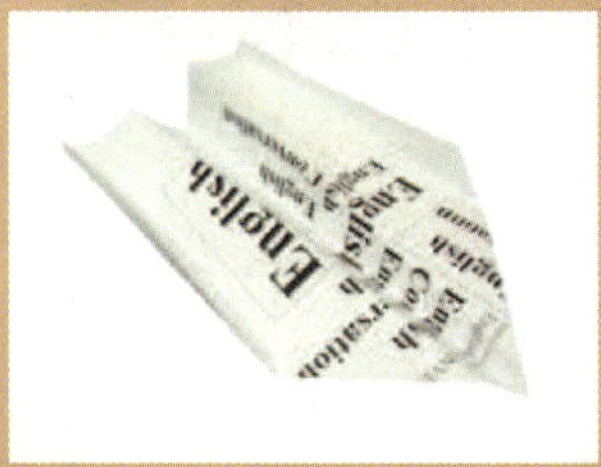

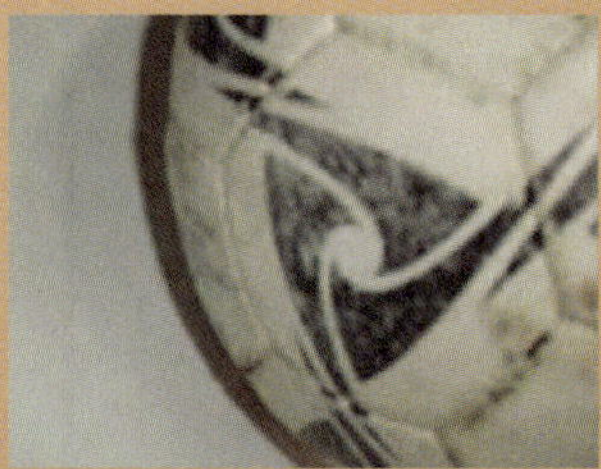

11: a) Fill in the missing information

Fill in the missing information by asking your friends some questions.

	Example	Friend 1	Friend 2	Friend 3
Name	Jess			
What kind of exercise do you enjoy?	Cardio.			
How often do you exercise?	Twice a week.			
What team ports do you like to play?	Soccer.			
Is aerobics fun?	No way.			

A) What kind of exercise do you enjoy doing?
B) I really enjoy cardiovascular exercise.

A) How often would you say you exercise?
B) Oh. Twice a week usually.

11: b) Listening Comprehension T5

Fill in the missing information by listening to the conversations.

	Jeff	Matthew
How often does he exercise?		
What sport does he think is the most fun?		
Does he do any cardio exercise?		

12: a) Write your own conversation (What sports are fun?)

Write a conversation wherein you ask someone what kind of sports s/he thinks are fun, then ask her/him how often s/he does exercise and what kind of exercise s/he does.

A) ______________________________

B) ______________________________

A) ______________________________

B) ______________________________

A) ______________________________

B) ______________________________

A) ______________________________

B) ______________________________

Now act out the conversations you wrote with your group members. Remember to involve all group members.

12: b) Write your own conversation (Would you like to ..?)

Write a conversation wherein you ask someone to come and join you in doing a particular sport, then act it out with your group.

A) ______________________________

B) ______________________________

A) ______________________________

B) ______________________________

A) ______________________________

B) ______________________________

A) ______________________________

B) ______________________________

"Would you like to play some tennis with me?"

12: c) Discussing Sports

Write a conversation wherein you and a friend talk about any given sport or exercise.

____

____

____

____

____

____

____

____

13) Puzzle

Use the sentences found in Unit 9 to help you complete the following puzzle.

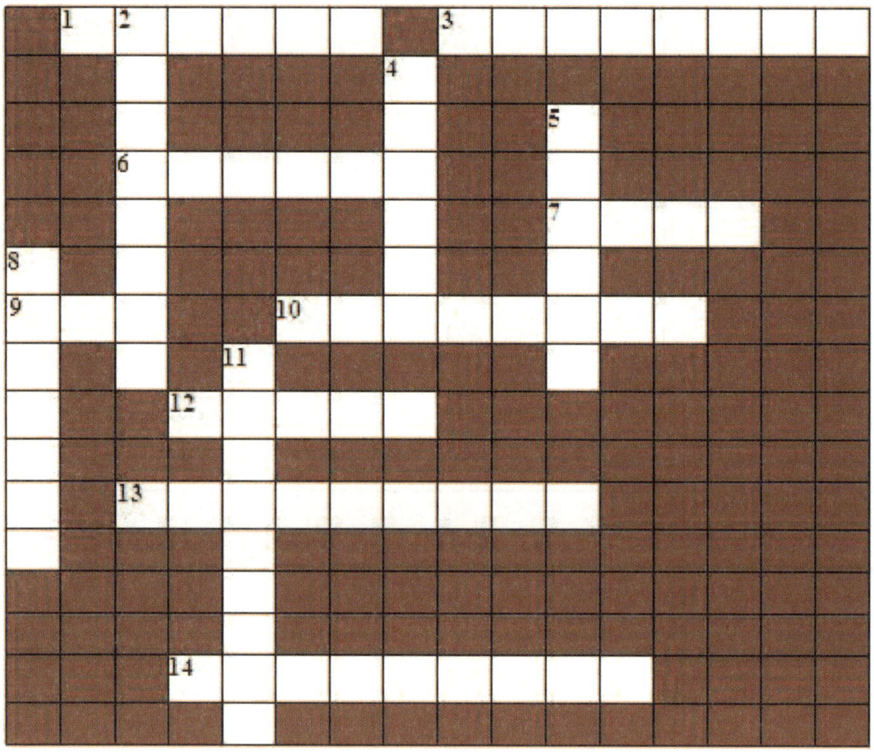

After you have completed the puzzle, check the 'Puzzle Solutions' section at the back of the book for the solution to the above puzzle.

Across

1) Table ________ is popular in China.

3) Suit ____________.

6) I don't have a tennis ____________.

7) Jumping ________ is boring.

9) Let's work on our ______.

10) ______________ is good exercise.

12) Are you up for a ________ then?

13) ____________ are sometimes heavy.

14) I'd like to do _____________ fun.

Down

2) I'd like to do some ___________.

4) You play so much _________ than me.

5) Soccer is good _________ exercise.

8) What are we __________ for?

11) Let's play some _______________.

BUSINESS NAME

Unit 10

The Day After Tomorrow

Grammar

Content

- The conjunction 'If'
- Expressing 'Future Tense' with the 'Present Continuous'

Unit breakdown:

Waiting For The Bus	p. 80
I'm going to go out.	p. 81
The Varieties of Tenses	p. 82
I'm going to the market.	p. 83
Comprehension Activities	p. 84
Review Activities	p. 85
Puzzle	p. 86

Future Events

This unit focuses on ...

- The varieties of Future Tense
- Future Tense Interrogatives
- Talking about future events
- Speaking in Future Tense
- Conditional Clauses

Catching The Bus

1) Waiting For The Bus

A) The bus is really late today.
B) Don't worry, it's going to come.

A) I really hope so.
B) It will be here in a few minutes.

A) I'll be late for school if the bus doesn't come soon.
B) I'll be late too then.

A) Oh good. Here it comes now.
B) See. I told you.

I'll be = I will be

Now practice the above conversation within your group. Use your own scenarios and say them out loud in English. Don't forget to involve all group members.

"I'll be a good boy. I promise."

2) Will you buy any ice cream?

A) Where are you going to go today Mom?
B) I am going shopping.
A) What will you buy?
B) I'm buying some groceries.
A) Will you buy some ice cream?
A) Maybe.
B) I'll be a really good boy if you do.
A) Do you promise?
B) Yes. I won't do anything silly. I promise.
A) OK. I'll get you some ice cream then.
B) Thank you mommy.

Now practice the above conversation within your group. Use your own scenarios and say them out loud in English. Don't forget to include all group members.

---

3) Listen to The Conversation T1

- Will you stop at every red light?
- Sure mom.
- I'm going to worry, so be careful.
- Don't worry mom.

4) I'll be taking the subway tonight. T2

A) I'll be going out with my friends tonight?

B) Where will you be going Mikyung?

A) I'll be going to Sinchon with my friends.

B) Will you be staying out late?

A) Yes. I'll be back tomorrow morning though.

B) OK. But be careful. I'm going to worry.

A) Don't worry mom. I'll take care of myself.

B) I'll see you tomorrow then.

Now practice the above conversation within your group. Use your own scenarios and say them out loud in English. Don't forget to involve all group members.

5) Comprehension Activity

		Yes	No
1)	Is Mikyung going to take the subway to Sinchon?	□	□
2)	Is she going to go home the same day?	□	□
3)	Is she going to get home the next morning?	□	□
4)	Is Mikyung's mother going to worry?	□	□
5)	Will Mikyung's mother go out with her?	□	□
6)	Is Mikyung going out alone.	□	□

"Will you stay out late?"

"Yes, but don't worry."

6) I'll be dancing all night long.

Q **What will you do tonight?**

A **I'll be dancing all night long.**

Q **What kind of music will you dance to?**

A **I'll dance to Classic Rock .**

Q **Will you be drinking?**

A **Yes, I will, but I won't drink any alcohol.**

Now practice the above conversation within your group. Use your own scenarios and say them out loud in English. Don't forget to involve all group members.

Will
Going to
I'll
It'll
I will

7) Future Tense Forms

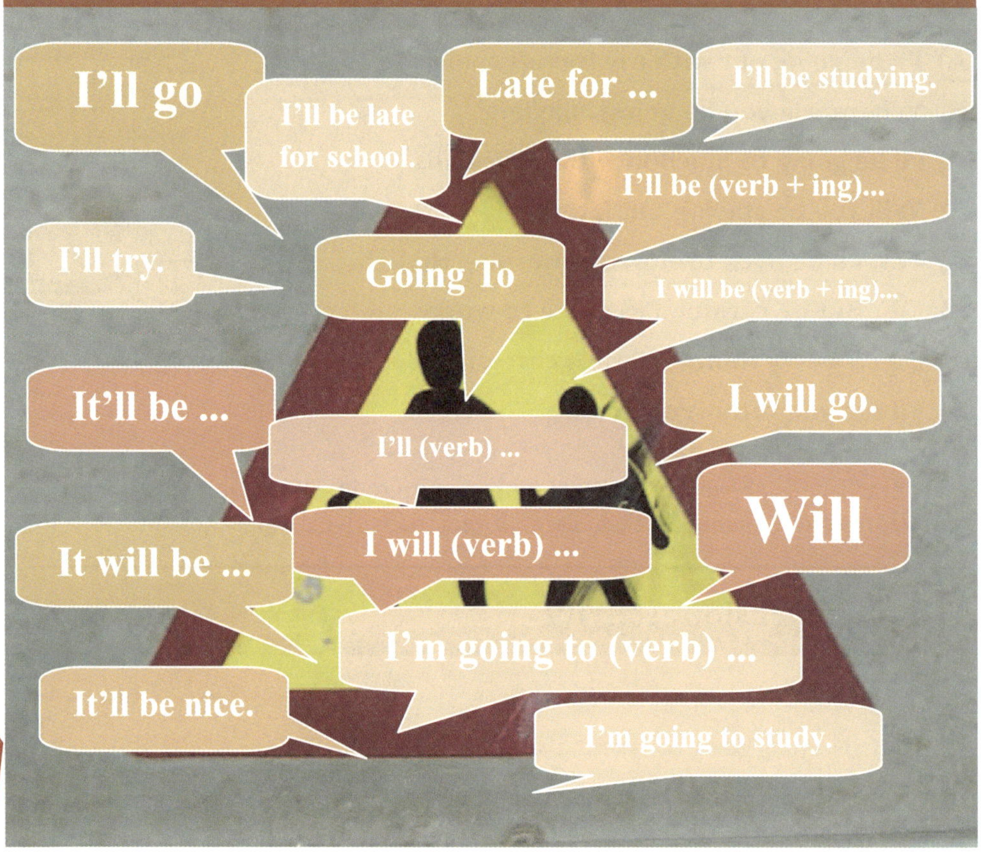

Now practice the above illustrated tenses. It is important that you know how to use and understand all of them. Don't forget to involve all group members.

8: a) Will this light ever change? T3

A) Be patient. The light will turn green soon.

B) Yes, but I have no time to wait.

A) Don't worry. You won't be late.

B) Is this light ever going to change?

A) It's going to change soon. Trust me.

B) Oh finally, it's green.

A) See!

B) I'll see ya later. I gotta run.

gotta = (have) got to
ya = you *[non standard]*

Now practice the above conversation within your group. Use your own scenarios and say them out loud in English. Don't forget to involve all group members.

8: b) I'm going to the market. T4

A) What are you doing tomorrow?

B) I'm going to the market.

A) What are you getting?

B) Some fruit and vegetables.

A) Are you making vegetable soup?

B) No. I simply like to have my fridge stacked.

A) I'll see you later then.

B) Yes. Bye.

Now ask your group members some questions. Use the conversation in activity 8 as a model for your conversations.

9) I'm buying fish.

A) What will you buy at the market?

B) I'm getting some fish.

A) What are you cooking?

B) I am making some Fish & Chips.

A) I'm sure it will be delicious.

B) Yes. I hope it will be.

"I'm getting some fish."

Now take the given conversation and model your own conversations on it. Once again use your own scenarios.

10) Fill in the missing information

What are you doing tomorrow?	What are you doing tomorrow?
I'm going to school.	
What'll you do on your next holiday?	**What'll you do on your next holiday?**
I'm travelling to Canada.	

Now take turns filling in the missing information by asking your friends some questions.

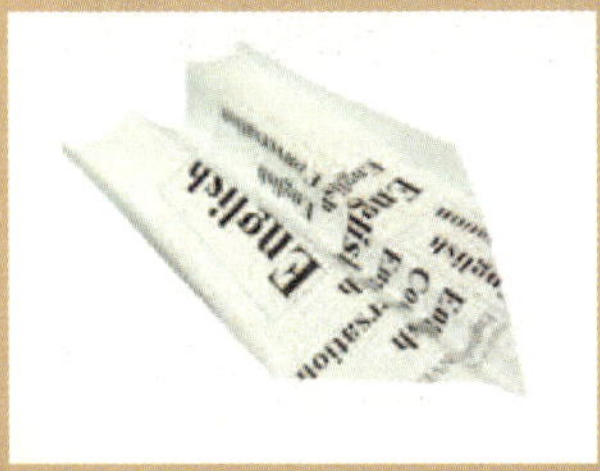

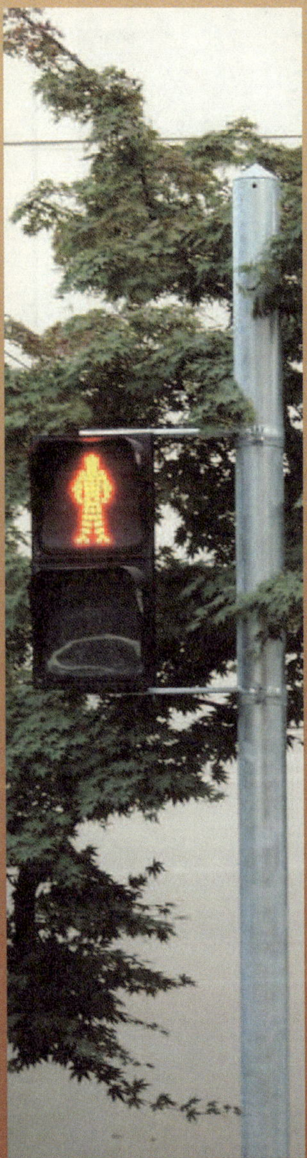

11: a) Fill in the missing information

Fill in the missing information by asking your friends some questions.

	Example	Friend 1	Friend 2	Friend 3
Name	Sam			
What will you do tonight, after work/ school?	I'll go to the movies.			
What'll you do tomorrow morning?	I will get ready for school?			
Will you do homework tonight?	No. I have no homework.			

A) What do you plan on doing after school today?
B) I'll be going to the movies with my girlfriend.

A) Will you be doing homework tonight?
B) No. I don't have any homework today.

11: b) Listening Comprehension T5

Fill in the missing information by listening to the conversations.

	May	Pamela
What will she be doing tonight?		
What is she going to do on the weekend?		
Will she travel abroad soon?		

12: a) Write your own conversation (What will you do ..?)

Write a conversation wherein you ask someone what s/he's going to do tonight.

A) ____________________

B) ____________________

A) ____________________

B) ____________________

A) ____________________

B) ____________________

A) ____________________

B) ____________________

Now act out the conversations you wrote with your group members. Remember to involve all group members.

12: b) Write your own conversation (What will you do on ..?)

Write a conversation wherein you ask someone what s/he plans on doing on the weekend?

A) ____________________

B) ____________________

A) ____________________

B) ____________________

A) ____________________

B) ____________________

A) ____________________

B) ____________________

"Do you have any plans for the weekend?"

12: c) Will you ... at/on ...?

Write a conversation wherein you ask someone if s/he is going to do anything specific at any given time in the future?

____

____

____

____

____

____

____

13) Puzzle

Use the sentences found in Unit 10 to help you complete the following puzzle.

After you have completed the puzzle, check the 'Puzzle Solutions' section at the back of the book for the solution to the above puzzle.

Across

1) Don't ____________.

5) I'm going ___ take the subway.

6) Be ____________.

8) I _____ go shopping today.

9) __________ me.

10) Will ______ stop at the red light?

12) Where are you __________ to go today?

Down

2) I _______ hope so.

3) Will you be ________ out late?

4) I'll be __________ to rock music.

7) Will this light ______ change?

9) What are you going to do __________?

11) Oh __________, it's green.

BUSINESS NAME

Unit 11

The Day Before Yesterday

Grammar

Content

- Past Tenses
- Past Simple
- Present Progressive

Unit breakdown:

Simple Past p. 88

Present Progressive p. 89

Past Tenses p. 90

Our holiday was very nice p. 91

Comprehension Activities p. 92

Review Activities p. 93

Puzzle p. 94

Just Yesterday (In The Past)

This unit focuses on ...

- The Present Simple and The Present Progressive
- How to talk about things that happened yesterday
- Asking questions about past events
- Things that happened some time ago

Going To Church

1) I went to church.

A) What did you do on Sunday?
B) I went to church.

A) Did you go with your family?
B) Yes, I did.

A) How did you get to church?
B) We took the family van.

A) Did you drive?
B) No. My father did.

Now practice the above conversation within your group. Use your own scenarios and say them out loud in English. Don't forget to involve all group members.

"This church was built 100 years ago."

2) The church was built some time ago.

A) This church looks very old.
B) Yes, you are right. It was built 100 years ago.
A) Does your family come to church here?
B) Yes. Even my grandparents came here some time ago.
A) Wow. Can I join the next sermon?
B) Sure. You should come on Sunday.
A) I'll be here on Sunday then.

Now practice the above conversation within your group. Use your own scenarios and say them out loud in English. Don't forget to include all group members.

3) Listen to The Conversation T1

- Did you feed the cat this morning?
- No, I didn't. Did you?
- No, I didn't.
- Poor thing. Let's feed her now then.

4) Did you fill the car? T2

Maggie **What were you doing when I called you dear?**
Jonny **I was filling the car with gas.**
Maggie **Were you filling the car at Petro Canada?**
Jonny **Yes, dear. I was.**
Maggie **Did you pay much?**
Jonny **I paid 85 dollars.**
Maggie **That's a lot of money.**
Jonny **You know dear, gas is expensive these days.**

Now practice the above conversation within your group. Use your own scenarios and say them out loud in English. Don't forget to involve all group members.

"Did you pay much?"

5) Comprehension Activity

		Yes	No
1)	Did Maggie fill the car with gas?	☐	☐
2)	Did Jonny fill the car with gas?	☐	☐
3)	Did Jonny fill the car at Petro Canada?	☐	☐
4)	Did Jonny pay a lot of money for the gas?	☐	☐
5)	Did Maggie think the gas was cheap.	☐	☐
6)	Did Maggie say the gas was expensive?	☐	☐

"I paid 85 dollars."

6) Did you recharge the battery?

Q **Why did you not answer your cell phone?**
A **I was charging my batteries.**

Q **I was trying to get through but couldn't.**
A **Really? I'm sorry.**

Q **You should buy another battery.**
A **I'll buy an extra one today.**

Now practice the above conversation within your group. Use your own scenarios and say them out loud in English. Don't forget to involve all group members.

7) The Past Tenses

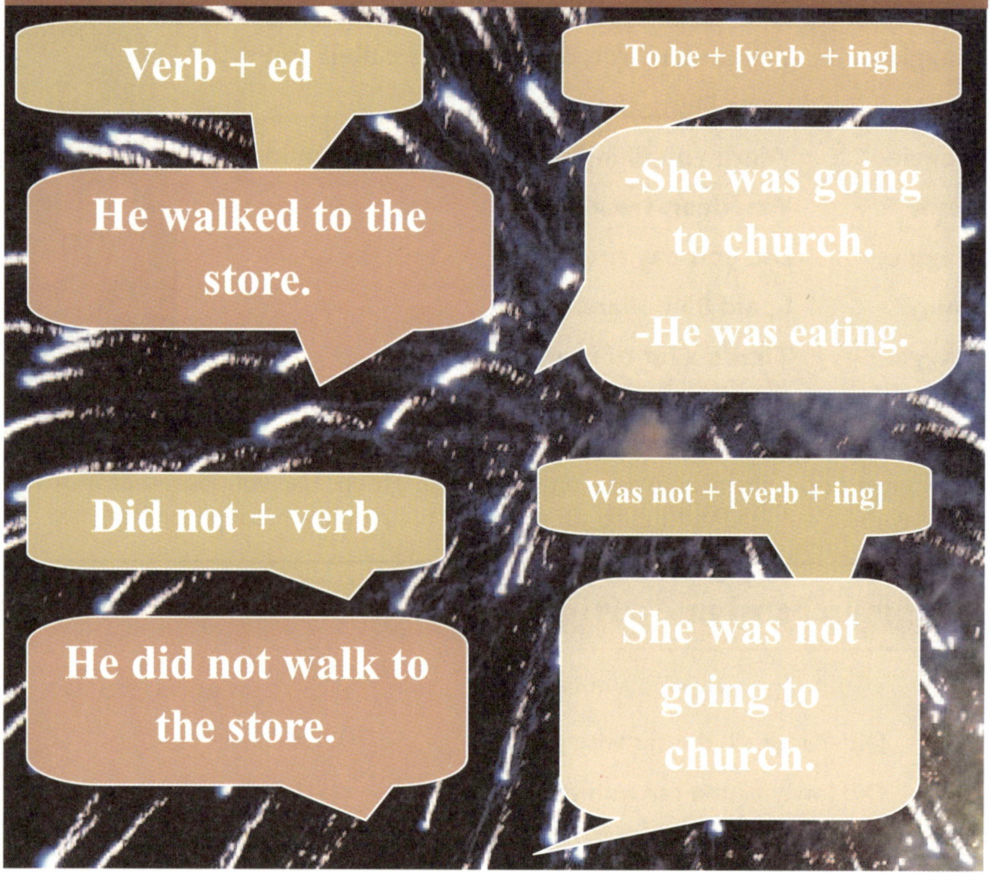

Now practice the above illustrated terms. It is important that you know how to use and understand all of them. Don't forget to involve all group members.

8: a) The fireworks were really nice last night. T3

A) Did you watch the fire works last night?

B) I sure did. Did you?

A) No, I was very busy.

B) What did you do?

A) I had to study for my final exam.

B) That's too bad.

A) Were the fireworks really nice?

B) Yeah, they were. The colors were really pretty.

Now practice the above conversation within your group. Use your own scenarios and say them out loud in English. Don't forget to involve all group members.

8: b) How was your trip to Canada? T4

A) How was your tip to Canada?

B) It was really fantastic.

A) Where did you go?

B) We went all around Ontario.

A) What was the most fun you had?

B) I guess it was when I was motorboating.

A) Is that so?

B) It was so scary and fun at the same time. I loved it when the boat was bouncing on the water.

Now ask your group members some questions. Use the conversation in activity 8 as a model for your conversations.

9) At The Motel

A) Did you stay at a nice motel?

B) Yes. It was very comfortable.

A) Will you go again?

B) Yes, I will. Here is a photo of it.

A) It looks cute.

B) Yeah, and the Muskoka Chairs were really comfy too.

A) You mean these yellow ones.

B) Yep.

Now take the given conversation and model your own conversations on it. Once again use your own scenarios.

"The Muskoka Chairs were really comfy."

10) Fill in the missing information

Where did you go last weekend?	Where did you go last weekend?
I went to my parent's house.	
Where did you go on your last vacation?	**Where did you go on your last vacation?**
We went to Los Angeles.	

Now take turns filling in the missing information by asking your friends some questions.

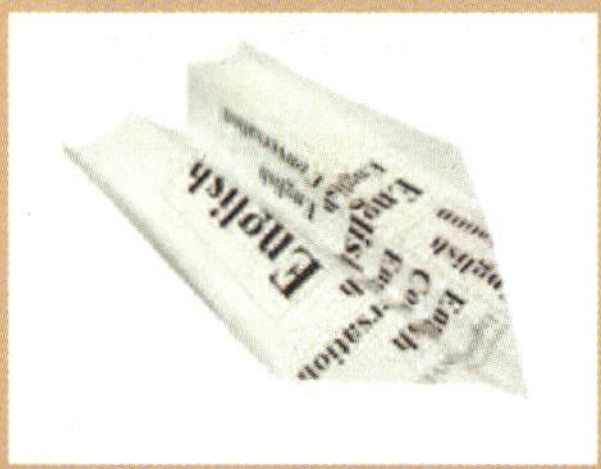

11: a) Fill in the missing information

Fill in the missing information by asking your friends some questions.

	Example	Friend 1	Friend 2	Friend 3
Name	Penny			
What did you do last night?	I went to Seoul.			
What did you do last weekend?	I played tennis.			
Did you do anything special last Christmas?	I cooked for my girlfriend.			

A) Could you tell me what you did last summer?
B) Yes. I went to Canada with my friend.

A) Did you do anything special last Christmas?
B) I played tennis with my husband.

11: b) Listening Comprehension T5

Fill in the missing information by listening to the conversations.

	Norbert	Stanley
What did he do last night?		
Did he watch TV last night?		
What did he do on the weekend?		

12: a) Write your own conversation (What did you do ..?)

Write a conversation wherein you ask someone what s/he did yesterday.

A) ______________________________

B) ______________________________

A) ______________________________

B) ______________________________

A) ______________________________

B) ______________________________

A) ______________________________

B) ______________________________

Now act out the conversations you wrote with your group members. Remember to involve all group members.

12: b) Write your own conversation (Could you tell me ..?)

Write a conversation wherein you ask someone what s/he did last Summer, then act it out with your group.

A) ______________________________

B) ______________________________

A) ______________________________

B) ______________________________

A) ______________________________

B) ______________________________

A) ______________________________

B) ______________________________

"Could you tell me what you did last Summer?"

12: c) What were you doing when I called you?

Write a conversation wherein you ask someone what s/he was doing at a specific time in the past.

____

____

____

____

____

____

____

13) Puzzle

Use the sentences found in Unit 11 to help you complete the following puzzle.

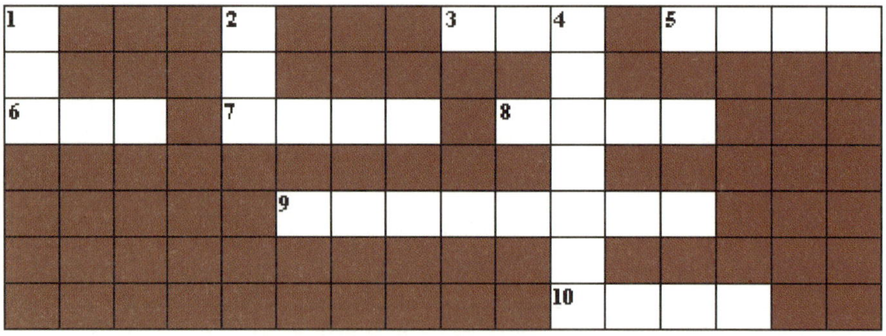

After you have completed the puzzle, check the 'Puzzle Solutions' section at the back of the book for the solution to the above puzzle.

Across

3) How ______ your trip to Canada?

5) What _______you doing when I called you?

6) What _______ you do on Saturday?

7) We _______ the family van.

8) Did you ________ the cat this morning?

9) I was _____________ my batteries.

10) Where did you go _________ weekend?

Down

1) This church looks very ______.

2) Why did you ______ answer your phone?

4) Did you do anything _________ last Christmas?

Unit 12

Clothing & Accessories

BUSINESS NAME

Grammar

Content

- The Conjunction 'But'
- The preposition 'With'

Unit breakdown:

Fashion Accessories	p. 96
Lending Money	p. 97
Accessory Terms	p. 98
Getting Some Assistance	p. 99
Comprehension Activities	p. 100
Review Activities	p. 101
Puzzle	p. 102

Shopping For Clothes

This unit focuses on …

- Fashion Accessories
- The Conjunction 'But'
- The Preposition 'With'
- Giving and receiving assistance while shopping

Necktie Tie

1) I need a new tie.

A) I really need a new tie.
B) Don't you have many ties already?

A) They are all old things.
B) How about this one then?

A) This green thing?
B) Sure. It suits you just fine.

A) I just don't know.
B) Try this one then.

it suit's you = it looks good on you

Now practice the above conversation within your group. Use your own scenarios and say them out loud in English. Don't forget to involve all group members.

"This tie looks good on you."

2) Let's buy a new tie.

A) How can I help you?
B) I'm looking for a nice tie.
A) OK. What do you think about this one?
B) How about that one?
A) Here you are. Would you like to try it on?
A) Yes, I'd like that.
B) Try it on with this shirt.
A) Do you have a white shirt?
B) Absolutely.
A) I'll try them on together then.
B) The fitting rooms are over there.

Now practice the above conversation within your group. Use your own scenarios and say them out loud in English. Don't forget to include all group members.

---

3) Listen to The Conversation T1

- This belt looks really nice.
- Buy it then.
- It's kind of expensive.
- You only live once you know. Just buy it.

4) This jacket looks good on you. T2

A) **Blake. This jacket looks good on you.**

B) **I do like it, but it's a little expensive.**

A) **Yes, but it's very nice.**

B) **I can't afford it though.**

A) **I'll lend you some money. You can pay me back later.**

B) **That's nice of you. Thank you.**

A) **Not a problem. That's what friends are for.**

B) **You're very kind, Heather.**

Now practice the above conversation within your group. Use your own scenarios and say them out loud in English. Don't forget to involve all group members.

5) Comprehension Activity

		True	False
1)	Blake thinks the jacket looks good on Heather.	□	□
2)	Heather thinks the Jacket looks good on Blake.	□	□
3)	Heather thinks the jacket is expensive.	□	□
4)	Blake can't afford the jacket.	□	□
5)	Heather does not want to lend Blake any money.	□	□
6)	Blake thinks Heather is very kind.	□	□

6) These are a dirty old pair of jeans.

Q **These are a dirty old pair of jeans.**

A **No, they aren't. They are brand new.**

Q **They look so dirty though.**

A **This is the style of the jeans.**

Q **You mean they are made to look this way?**

A **They sure are.**

Now practice the above conversation within your group. Use your own scenarios and say them out loud in English. Don't forget to involve all group members.

7) Accessory Terms

Now practice the above illustrated terms. It is important that you know how to use and understand all of them. Don't forget to involve all group members.

8: a) This shirt and this tie look good together. T3

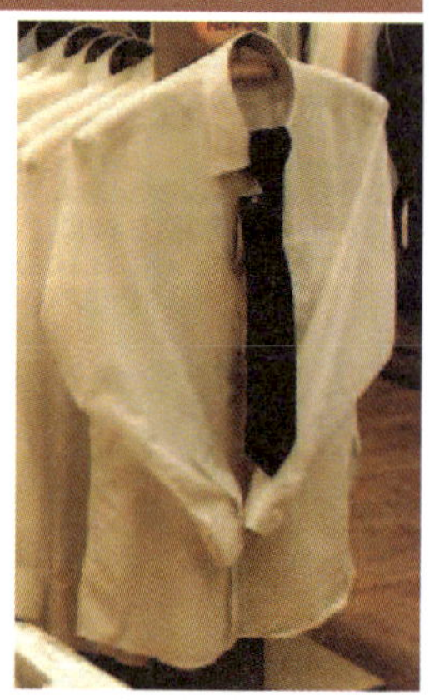

A) This white shirt and this black tie look really good together.

B) This blue tie is much better with that shirt.

A) I think I like this black one better though.

B) All right. You'll have to wear it.

A) I'll try it on. Where is the fitting room?

B) It's over there.

A) I'll be right back.

B) OK. I'll be here waiting.

Now practice the above conversation within your group. Use your own scenarios and say them out loud in English. Don't forget to involve all group members.

8: b) New Shoes T4

A) How may I assist you?

B) I'd like a new pair of shoes please.

A) What size are you looking for?

B) Size 8.

A) I have this in size 8. It's really nice.

B) May I try it on?

A) Certainly. Let me get a new pair for you.

B) Thank you.

Now ask your group members some questions. Use the conversation in activity 8 as a model for your conversations.

9) Winter Clothes

A) I need some winter clothes.

B) Would you like a scarf and a hat?

A) No. I'd like to buy a new coat.

B) Here is a nice one for you.

A) I like that one better.

B) Would you like to try it on?

A) Yes, please.

B) The fitting room is over there.

"I'd like to buy a new coat for winter."

Now take the given conversation and model your own conversations on it. Use your own scenarios.

10) Fill in the missing information

What kind of clothes would you like to buy? *I'd like to buy a new coat.* **What is your favourite color for clothes?** *I like to wear white the most.*	**What kind of clothes would you like to buy?** **What is your favourite color for clothes?**

Now take turns filling in the missing information by asking your friends some questions.

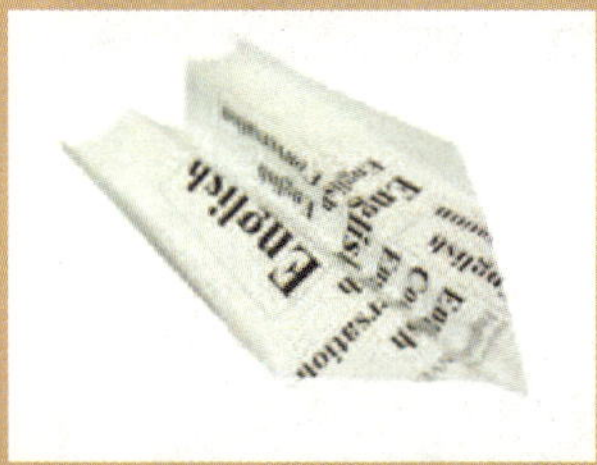

11: a) Fill in the missing information

Fill in the missing information by asking your friends some questions.

	Example	Friend 1	Friend 2
Name	Tim		
Do you like wearing a shirt and tie?	I hate wearing a shirt and tie.		
Do you think you look good in blue jeans?	I think I look great in blue jeans.		
What kind of clothes would you like to buy then?	I'd love to buy a sports jacket.		

A) Do you like wearing a shirt and a tie?
B) Yes. I love wearing a shirt and tie.

A) What kind of clothes would you like to buy?
B) I'd like to buy some casual clothes.

11: b) Listening Comprehension T5

Fill in the missing information by listening to the conversation.

	Justin	Pierre
Does he like wearing a shirt and tie?		
Does he think he looks good in blue jeans?		
What color of clothes does he like to wear?		

12: a) Write your own conversation (How may I help you?)

Write a conversation wherein you go into a store and are asked if you needed any assistance.

A) ______________________________

B) ______________________________

A) ______________________________

B) ______________________________

A) ______________________________

B) ______________________________

A) ______________________________

B) ______________________________

Now act out the conversations you wrote with your group members. Remember to involve all group members.

12: b) Write your own conversation (What kind of ...?)

Write a conversation wherein you ask someone what kinds of clothes s/he thinks s/he looks good in, then act it out with your group.

"What kind of clothes would you say you look good in?"

A) ______________________________

B) ______________________________

A) ______________________________

B) ______________________________

A) ______________________________

B) ______________________________

A) ______________________________

12: c) Could I try this on?

Write a conversation wherein you are wanting to try something on in the fitting room.

____

____

____

____

____

____

____

13) Puzzle

Use the sentences found in Unit 12 to help you complete the following puzzle.

After you have completed the puzzle, check the 'Puzzle Solutions' section at the back of the book for the solution to the above puzzle.

Across

1) I have many ties __________.

4) I can't __________ it though.

7) This __________ you just fine.

8) __________ Room

9) Let me get a new ________ for you.

10) This jacket __________ good on you.

11) They're __________ new.

Down

2) I'm __________ for a nice belt.

3) I like that one __________.

5) That's what __________ are for.

6) This shirt and this tie look good __________.

Hidden Tape Scripts:

Unit 1

T5

A) What's your name?
B) My name is Peter.
A) What's your last name, Peter?
B) My last name is Washington.
A) How do you spell that?
B) W-A-S-H-I-N-G-T-O-N
A) What's your student number?
B) My student number is 567-324-982.
A) And how old are you?
B) I'm 13 years old.
A) Thank you, Peter.
B) You're welcome.

A) What's your name?
B) I'm Robert.
A) It's good to meet you, Robert.
B) It's good to meet you, too.
A) Can you tell me your last name?
B) It's Merchant.
A) Can you spell that for me?
B) M-E-R-C-H-A-N-T
A) All right. Can you give me your student number, please?
B) 134-654-765
A) How old are you?
B) Eleven.
A) Thank you, Robert.
B) You are welcome.

Unit 2

T5

A) Good day, Margaret.
B) Hello there.
A) What do you do, Margaret?
B) I am a student.
A) A student? Are you a college student?
B) No, I am a student at Bridgeways School of English.
A) Really? How many hours a week do you study?
B) I study around 28 hours a week.
A) Thank you, Margaret.
B) Not a problem.

A) Hi, Suzy.
B) Hi, Justin.
A) Suzy, can you tell me what you do?
B) Yes. I am a nurse.
A) Do you work in a hospital?
B) Yes. I work at Seoul National University Hospital.
A) Can you also tell us how many hours a week you work?
B) Sure. I work 40 hours a week.
A) Well, thank you, Suzy.
B) You're welcome.

Unit 3

T5

A) Hi, Homer.
B) Hello.
A) Homer, do you like your job?
B) Yes, I do.
A) Why do you like your job, Homer?
B) Because, it's very challenging. You see, I am a fireman.
A) What would you like to do for a living?
B) What do you mean? I am a fireman.
A) Well, what's your dream job?
B) I love being a fireman. I wouldn't change it for the world, so my dream job is to be a fireman.

A) Hello there, Tony.
B) Hello to you, too.
A) Tony. Would you tell us whether you like your school or not?
B) Not really.
A) Why not?
B) Because my teachers give us too much homework.
A) OK. What is your dream job?
B) I'd like to be a politician I guess.
A) A politician?
B) Yes. I'd like to be the Prime Minister of England.

Unit 4

T5 At the Restaurant (Brian)

A) Welcome to Joe's Sandwich Shop. I'm your waitress Angela. What would you like to order today?
B) I'd like to order the American Burger with French Fries.
A) I'm sorry, but it's not available at the moment.
B) Could I have the Bacon Lettuce Tomato Sandwich then?
A) Sure. Anything to drink with that?
B) Could I have a can of cola?

At the Restaurant (Jamie)

A) Welcome to The Texas Ranch Steak House. Are you ready to order?
B) Yes. Could I order the T-Bone Steak with the Baked Potato?
A) I am sorry, we are out of T-Bone Steaks.
B) I see. Do you have the Beef Steak with the Baked Potato then?
A) Yes. Would you like a drink with that?
B) I'd like a bottle of mineral water please.
A) Sure. Your order will take a few minutes.

Unit 5

T5

A) How much money do you have, Bob?
B) I don't have much money. I only have 26 dollars.
A) Well, Bob. Is that all in bills?
B) No, it's not. It's all in quarters. You know, 25 cent coins.
A) I could use some change for the bus. Will you lend me some change?
B) Sure. How much do you need?
A) A dollar twenty five.

A) Hi, Jerry.
B) Hi there.
A) Jerry. Could I ask you how much money you have?
B) Sure. But I can't lend you any money if that's what you're after.
A) OK.
B) As you can see, I only have this one dollar bill in my pocket.
A) Are you broke?
B) No. I use my debit card to pay for everything. This one dollar bill here is for the bus.

Unit 6

T5

A) Roger, what is your travel destination this weekend?
B) I am going to Hollywood, California.
A) How long will you be staying in Hollywood?
B) I'll be there Saturday and Sunday. So two days in total.
A) How are you getting there Roger?
B) I am driving.
A) Thank you.
B) Not a problem.

A) Rafael. Where are you going this Christmas vacation?
B) I am visiting my parents in New York City.
A) And how long do you plan on staying?
B) I am staying till New Year's Day. So that's10 days all together.
A) Wonderful. Now, are you going by bus.
B) No. It takes too long by bus. I'm flying.
A) Great! Thank you, Rafael.
B) Sure.

Unit 7

T5

A) Jeremy, could you tell us if you own a high definition television?
B) Yes, I do, Bob.
A) How about a Playstation 3? Do you own one of those?
B) No, Bob. I do own an XBox 360 though.
A) Well, that's close enough I guess. Thank you, Jeremy.
B) You're welcome, Bob.

A) Brad, I was wondering whether you own an HD TV?
B) No, I don't. I do have a projector though.
A) Do you watch TV on the projector?
B) Yes, I do.
A) Do you own a Playstation 3?
B) No, but I have a Playstation 2 console.
A) So, you probably don't have an XBox then.
B) No. I do have an XBox as well.

Unit 8

T5

A) Hi, Jackie.
B) Well, hello there.
A) Jackie, could you tell us what movie genres you like?
B) I like all kinds of movies, but I guess my favourite kind of movies are romantic comedies.
A) Now, I have a question about games. Have you ever played the crane game?
B) Yes, I have, but I didn't win anything.
A) All right Jackie. Thank you for answering my questions.
B) You're welcome.

A) Cathy, what kind of movie genre do you like?
B) I don't like any kind of movies. Movies are too long and boring.
A) Well, that certainly is a surprise.
I do have a couple more questions for you. Did you ever play the crane game?
B) Sure. I play it all the time.
A) Have you ever won anything?
B) Oh gosh yes. I won teddy bears, a silver ring, candy and all kinds of other stuff.
A) Well. I thank you for your patience, Cathy. Goodbye.
B) Bye bye.

Unit 9

T5

A) Jeff, how often would you say you exercise?
B) I guess I exercise around 2 times a week. Yes, about twice a week.
A) What sports are most fun for you, Jeff?
B) I really like soccer. Yes, soccer is a lot of fun.
A) Do you do any cardio exercise?
B) Well, I do run a lot when I play soccer, so yes, I suppose I do.
A) Thank you for taking the time to answer my questions.

A) Matthew, I have a few questions for you.
B) OK.
A) Matthew, how often do you exercise?
B) Every day.
A) Wow. That's really amazing.
B) Well. Not really.
A) What sports would you consider to be fun?
B) I really love playing tennis. It's good cardio exercise.

Unit 10

T5

A) May, would you mind telling us what you'll be doing tonight?
B) I think I am going to watch some television.
A) How about this weekend?
B) This weekend I'll be visiting my parents.
A) Do your parents live nearby?
B) Not really. They live across the boarder in the USA.
A) Thank you, May.
B) You're welcome.

A) Pamela, can you tell us what you're doing tonight?
B) Yes. I am meeting friends for dinner.
A) Are you eating out?
B) We are eating at an Italian buffet.
A) What are you doing this weekend?
B) I'm going for a hike in the mountains.
A) Good then. That concludes my questions. I appreciate you taking your time.
B) It's no bother really.

Unit 11

T5

A) Norbert, what did you do last night?
B) I had dinner with my girlfriend.
A) Did you watch TV at all?
B) Yes, a little.
A) What did you do on the weekend?
B) I relaxed all weekend.
A) That sounds nice.

A) Hi, Stanley.
B) Hello there.
A) What did you do last night?
B) I visited my friend.
A) What did you do with your friend?
B) We had a few drinks and watched TV.
A) Did you watch any TV on the weekend too?
B) No. I went to the beach.

Unit 12

T5

A) Justin, do you like wearing a shirt and tie?
B) I really don't like wearing that stuff.
A) Do you think you look good in blue jeans then?
B) Yes, I believe I look good in blue jeans.
A) What color of clothes do you like to wear?
B) I like wearing navy blue clothes.
A) OK then. That's all the questions I have for you today. Thank you for your time.

A) Hi, Pierre. Can I bother you with just a few questions?
B) OK. Go ahead.
A) Do you like wearing a shirt and tie?
B) Yes, of course. I look good in a shirt and tie.
A) Do you think you look good in jeans?
B) Not really.
A) What is your favourite color for clothes?
B) I really love black.
A) Thank you, Pierre.
B) No worries.

Puzzle Solutions

Unit 1

Across

2) first
3) number
6) later
7) like
8) How
10) years
11) student

Down

1) welcome
2) free
4) meet
5) pleasure
9) around

Unit 2

Across

3) long
5) hours
7) doing
9) faster
10) driving
11) going

Down

1) plans
2) company
4) getting
6) commute
8) living

Unit 3

Across

3) dream
4) work
5) homemaker
6) pilot
8) singer
10) Because
11) kidding

Down

1) enjoy
2) company
3) does
7) job
9) living

Unit 4

Across

5) about
6) order
7) with
8) idea
10) How
11) ready
12) try
13) special
15) think

Down

1) sounds
2) delicious
3) would
4) unhealthy
9) really
14) coming

Unit 5

Across

1) expensive
5) borrow
6) change
7) purchase
8) buy
9) bills
10) money

Down

2) pretty
3) dollars
4) Bank
8) broke

Unit 6

Across

2) by
3) Hop
6) would
7) takes
8) dangerous
9) cheaper
10) travelling
11) staying
13) expensive
14) destination

Down

1) fast
4) comfortable
5) better
12) getting

Unit 7

Across

2) Phone
3) Screen
6) Definition
8) volume
10) over
Cellular

Down

1) quality
4) control
5) use
6) Digital
7)
9) own

Unit 8

Across

1) choose
2) action
4) crane
headphones
6) movie
8) console
9) then
10) genre

Down

1) Comedy
3) choice
5)
7) video

Unit 9

Across

1) tennis
3) yourself
6) racket
7) rope
9) abs
10) Aerobics
12) match
13) Dumbbells
14) something

Down

2) exercise
4) better
5) cardio
8) waiting
11) badminton

Unit 10

Across

1) worry
5) to
6) patient
8) will
9) Trust
10) you
12) going

Down

2) really
3) staying
4) dancing
7) ever
9) tomorrow
11) finally

Unit 11

Across

3) was
5) were
6) did
7) took
8) feed
9) charging
10) last

Down

1) old
2) not
4) special

Unit 12

Across

1) already
4) afford
7) suits
8) Fitting
9) pair
10) looks
11) brand

Down

2) looking
3) better
5) friends
6) together

Complimentary Activity

A) This activity is a complementary activity for activity 10) on page 35.

MENU

French Fries	American Hamburger	Crepes
Pan Fried Sausages	Meat Pie	Goulash
Fried Chicken	Sweet and Sour Pork	Mexican Chilli

Supplementary Writing Activity

Write a few lines about the Bridgeways 2 course. Write your own thoughts.

Explain to your teacher why you think you would recommend the Bridgeways 2 English language course to other students who would like to learn English. What is the single most important reason for this recommendation? Why would you want to study from the Bridgeways 3 English language course? Also, make a list of what you learned from the Bridgeways 2 EL course.

Irregular Verbs

Base Form	Past Simple
be	was/were
beat	beat
become	became
begin	began
bend	bent
bet	bet
bite	bit
blow	blew
break	broke
bring	brought
build	built
buy	bought
can	could
cast	cast
catch	caught
choose	chose
come	came
cost	cost
cut	cut
do	did
dig	dug
draw	drew
drink	drank
drive	drove
eat	ate
fall	fell
feed	fed
feel	felt
fight	fought
find	found
fit	fit
fly	flew
forget	forgot
freeze	froze
get	got
give	gave
go	went
grow	grew
hang	hung
have	had
hear	heard
hide	hid
hit	hit
hurt	hurt
keep	kept

Base Form	Past Simple
know	knew
leave	left
lend	lent
let	let
light	lit
lose	lost
make	made
mean	meant
meet	met
must	had to
pay	paid
put	put
read	read
ride	rode
ring	rang
rise	rose
run	ran
say	said
see	saw
sell	sold
send	sent
set	set
shake	shook
shine	shone
shut	shut
sing	sang
sit	sat
sleep	slept
speak	spoke
spend	spent
stand	stood
steal	stole
stick	stuck
sweep	swept
swim	swam
take	took
teach	taught
tell	told
think	thought
throw	threw
understand	understood
wake	woke
wear	wore
win	won
write	wrote

Guide to Using Bridgeways.

It is important to realize that all sentence structures can be recycled by substituting certain words or phrases within the structures themselves. The order must be left the same while substituting, for the most part, nouns, noun phrases, verbs and adjectives.

See the following sentence for example:

I like watching television <u>at night</u>.

In the above sentence, the prepositional phrase **'at night'** can be substituted with other prepositional phrases that also depict time.

For example:

I like watching television *in the morning*.

Furthermore, the object **'television'** can be substituted by other nouns that go with the gerund **'watching'**. These verbs would include; news, movies, films documentaries and the likes.

For example:

I like watching *the news* in the morning.

Moreover, the gerund **'watching'** can be switched out as well.

For example:

I like *listening* to the news in the morning.

By substituting the entire non-finite clause **'listening to the news'**, we can begin to describe other types of activities one might find oneself engage in.

For example:

I like *playing tennis* in the morning.

Even the transitive verb **'like'** can be substituted.

For example:

I *hate* playing tennis in the morning.

And lastly, the subject 'I' can be substituted with other pronouns.

For example:

***She* hates playing tennis in the morning.**

Of course, in the case of the above sentence, one must not forget to conjugate the verb **'hate'** by attaching the **'s'** to the end; **'hates'**.

All in all, substitution charts make the process of substitution relatively easy since the grammatical elements that can be substituted are already isolated for the learner.

For example:

<table>
<tr><td rowspan="2">I</td><td>like</td><td>watching</td><td>television</td><td>at night.</td></tr>
<tr><td>love</td><td>listening to</td><td>music</td><td>in the morning.</td></tr>
<tr><td>She</td><td>hates</td><td>playing</td><td>tennis</td><td>during the day.</td></tr>
<tr><td>We</td><td>prefer</td><td>learning</td><td>English</td><td>using substitution charts.</td></tr>
</table>

In the first level of the Bridgeways series, the use of substitution charts is prevalent, however, in the following levels (Bridgeways 2 & 3) the use of substitution charts is limited, since learners at these levels are expected to rely less on substitution charts for support. Although, level 2 of the Bridgeways series does provide learners with some degree of support via substitution charts, they are phased out in later units, although underlined sections do, at times, bring to the attention of learners that they are interchangeable parts of sentences that can and should be substituted. In essence, learners will not have such support in real life, therefore, it is essential that such support mechanisms are avoided all together at more advanced levels.

Consider the following conversation as an example.

A) Excuse me. What's your name?

B) My name is Diane Southerland.

A) Is Southerland your last name?

B) Yes, it is.

A) Can you spell that for me?

B) S-O-U-T-H-E-R-L-A-N-D

A) Thank you. Now, can I have your phone number please?

B) Yes, it's 0-1-2-4-5-6-7-8-9-0.

A) Thank you Diane.

B) You are most welcome.

See how certain elements of the entire conversation can be substituted in the following example.

A) Excuse me. What's your name?

B) My name is ***Tom Bullock.***

A) Is ***Bullock*** your last name?

B) Yes, it is.

A) Can you spell that for me?

B) ***B-U-L-L-O-C-K***

A) Thank you. Now, can I have your phone number please?

B) Yes, it's ***3-4-8-7-2-9-7-1-0-5.***

A) Thank you ***Tom***.

B) You are most welcome.

In the example below, other elements of the original example conversation are substituted to provide learners with yet another variation of the same conversation.

A) Excuse me **Peter**. What's your ***address***?

B) My ***address*** is ***27 Wellington Drive, Denver, Colorado***.

A) Is ***Denver*** your ***home state***?

B) Yes, it is.

A) Can you spell that for me?

B) ***D-E-N-V-E-R***

A) Thank you. Now, can I have your ***student number*** please?

B) Yes, it's ***756-789-365-234.***

A) Thank you **Peter.**

B) You are most welcome.

Attention Teachers!

The method of teaching English conversation, encapsulated by the Bridgeways series, has provided the author's learners with great success in improving their English conversation skills. After all, practice makes perfect, and this book provides ample opportunities for learners to put the English language to active conversational practice within the EFL classroom. It is this ample opportunity which promotes learners to acquire the spoken language skills necessary to hold everyday conversations via the English language.

More importantly, learners find the Bridgeways series interesting and fun. Nonetheless, teacher should always keep in mind that the group settings, of 4 to 5 individuals, the learners are placed in have the most effect if learners choose their own groups. It is important that learners do so since they become less hesitant in generating English conversation if they are grouped together with other learners they feel most comfortable with. It is best, however, to place at least one more capable learner in each of the groups if possible. It is left to the teacher's discretion as to how s/he deliberates on which learners are more capable than the others. Overall, the more capable learners have much to pass on to the less capable ones and often take the roles of motivators thus placing much of the onus of learning and acquiring into the learners' hands.

Within all EFL courses, teachers have a duty in guiding learners through the learning process. Without the careful guidance of the teacher, the journey to enlightenment is a daunting task for even the most able learner. It is this kind of guidance which is expected of all teachers, using the Bridgeways series, in teaching English conversation.

It is essential that teachers go over the 'Guide to Using Bridgeways' (p.116) with their students, before starting on Unit 1, since the Bridgeways EFL series becomes most effective, in facilitating classroom dialogue among the learners, if all activities are carried out in the manner in which they've been designed to be carried out in. Therefore, the teacher is charged with the responsibility to walk the learners through the processes of substitution in the illustrated conversations within the Bridgeways books, in order to allow the course to provide learners with the best opportunities to improve their English conversation skills. Of course, learners are expected to acquire the skill of substitution after the teacher has gone over the process and has assisted the learners a number of times, nonetheless, the teacher should, at all times, keep in mind that learners sometimes prefer taking the easy route, and thus it should become the teacher's responsibility to make sure the activities are carried out in the outlined manner on a consistent basis.

Paul Z. Jambor

Paul Z. Jambor has 11 years of experience teaching English as a foreign language in Hungary and Korea combined. He has been a foreign language professor at the university level for 6 years now. He has a Master of Arts in Teaching English as a Second/Foreign Language from the UK. Moreover he has undertaken extensive research in the field of English Language Teaching within the context of a Korean university setting, in order to determine the effectiveness of the 'Group Style' approach in teaching English as a foreign language. Through the course of his research Professor Jambor has come to the conclusion that the most effective way of teaching English conversation in the Korean university setting is to teach it in a group setting wherein students have ample means and opportunities to use the language via verbal practice. This method may seem simple in theory, however it is nevertheless tricky to implement in the foreign language classroom since most ES/FL books are not geared toward oral practice. Subsequently, the aim of this book is to provide a suitable classroom setting that encourages students to take active roles in verbal communication. Overall, this book is specifically designed for oral communication practice in a simple and comprehensive manner, so students do not feel overwhelmed with the challenges and pressures of learning a foreign language. In essence, this book is the very thing learners need for oral communicative development. The teaching approach encapsulated by this book is tried and tested by the author. By and large, the book is really the step in the right direction if the aim is to improve oral communicative competence.